VIOLENCE IN THE
NEW TESTAMENT

VIOLENCE IN THE
NEW TESTAMENT

EDITED BY

SHELLY MATTHEWS AND E. LEIGH GIBSON

t&t clark

NEW YORK • LONDON

T & T Clark International, Madison Square Park, 15 East 26th Street, New York, NY 10010
T & T Clark International, The Tower Building, 11 York Road, London SE1 7NX
T & T Clark International is a Continuum imprint.

Unless otherwise indicated, biblical quotations are from the New Revised Standard Version Bible, copyright 1989, Division of Christian Education of the National Council of the Churches of Christ in the United States of America. Used by permission. All rights reserved.

Cover art: Bibliothèque nationale de France

Cover design: Lee Singer

Library of Congress Cataloging-in-Publication Data

Violence in the New Testament / edited by Shelly Matthews and E. Leigh Gibson.
    p. cm.
  Includes bibliographical references and index.
  ISBN 0-567-02500-4 (pbk.)
  1. Violence in the Bible. 2. Bible. N.T.—Criticism, interpretation, etc. I. Gibson, E. Leigh.
II. Matthews, Shelly.
  BS2545.V55V56 2005
  225.8'3036—dc22

                              2004023677

Printed in the United States of America

05 06 07 08 09 10   10 9 8 7 6 5 4 3 2 1

CONTENTS

=====

ACKNOWLEDGMENTS

The editors wish to thank Tom Kazee, Vice President and Dean for Academic Affairs at Furman University, for his generous support of this project, and Evan Gatti for her gracious and expert assistance with the book's final details. Shelly Matthews would also like to thank her friend and colleague Vincent Hausmann for invaluable conversations about the intersection of violence and the sacred.

INTRODUCTION

═══

"Violence is the heart and secret soul of the sacred."

—*René Girard*

"The contradiction between the commandment to love and the incitement to hate not only belongs to later interpretations of the [Fourth] Gospel but is also inherent in the text itself."

—*Adele Reinhartz*

To say that the United States will never be the same after the attacks of September 11, 2001, has become something of a platitude, but not one without merit. The field of religious studies is no exception and has witnessed a flurry of publications documenting and exploring the relationship between religion and violence. However, when scholars of ancient Judaism and early Christianity engage such questions, they frequently attest to the persistence of a millennia-old bias: investigations of violence and the Bible all too commonly treat only the books of the Hebrew Bible or otherwise place the origins of "Judeo-Christian" violence squarely within Judaism. Marcion's second-century distinction between the God of the Old Testament as responsible for violence and vengeance and the God of the New Testament as a God of mercy and love looms large in the consciousness of the West.[1] In its largest scope, this book interrogates the assumption that the New Testament is a book solely of love, mercy, and peace, lying outside the web of religion and violence. Through its focus on *violence in* the New Testament, this volume situates itself within religious studies scholarship that sees violence as closely intertwined with religious experience, religious ritual, and religious expression. Through its focus on violence in the *New Testament,* it seeks to redress a serious gap in this scholarship by insisting that these foundational documents of Christianity are not somehow above the fray, but must also be scrutinized for their violent content and effects.

1

Therefore, we take seriously René Girard's insight that violence and religion are deeply interconnected and that one function of sacrificial religions may be to channel and to mask violent human impulses.[2] With Robert Orsi, we resist understandings of religion that cast it as concerned solely and essentially with a culture's positive and desirable qualities.[3] We ask with Elizabeth Castelli about the ways violence and truth are "irrevocably hard-wired together into the circuitry of our culture."[4] We build upon Regina Schwartz's study of the crucial role that monotheism plays in identity construction along the axis of us-them and ultimately violent action.[5] We draw on the work of social conflict theorists such as Vivienne Jabri, who understands conflict as a constructed discourse embedded in larger discursive and institutional webs.[6] The foundational work of postcolonial theorists, including Franz Fanon and Homi Bhabha, enable scholars in this volume to incorporate the dynamics of empire into analyses of religious violence.

With a lens sharpened by engagement with these larger theoretical questions of violence in religion, we focus here on texts of the New Testament. The issue of religious violence in canonical gospel, epistle, Apocalypse, and Acts alike has been underscrutinized in general, and—rather more inexplicably—neglected even in studies devoted specifically to violence "in the Bible." For example, a recent edition of *Religious Studies News,* an Internet journal of the Society of Biblical Literature, advertises itself as a feature on violence in the Bible, yet articles focus with virtual singularity on Hebrew Bible texts and Hebrew Bible atrocities.[7] Undoubtedly, the concepts of holy war and covenantal exclusion, along with the raped and dismembered women that litter the pages of Genesis, Judges, and Ezekiel, merit the attention they receive in this issue of *Religious Studies News.* But by raising questions only about Hebrew texts, this issue performs a sort of violence of its own—the "real" problem lies in the "Jewish" texts, not in the Christian Testament. In this regard, even Regina Schwartz's most recent study, *The Curse of Cain: The Violent Legacy of Monotheism,* also disappoints, for in spite of its broad subtitle, it highlights the violent legacy of Jewish monotheism, treating Christianity and Islam only in passing. Schwartz draws our attention to Cain and Abel; Moses and Joshua; David, Amnon, and Tamar; but not to the Apostle Paul's violent desires, or the Gospel of Matthew's depiction of tortured slaves, or the fiery and forceful Son of God sitting in judgment in Revelation. That is, Christianity could be read in this study merely as a conduit for the violent legacy of Jewish monotheism and not as a player in generating conflict and violence as it refines and recasts Jewish monotheism to its own ends.

More troubling than studies of violence in the Bible that ignore the New Testament are those that lift up the New Testament as somehow containing the antidote for Old Testament violence. This is ultimately the case, for instance, in the work of Girard, who embedded his views on mimetic violence and scapegoating in a general theory of religion and culture that he crowned with a triumphalist reading of Christian Scripture.[8] Girard's theorizing triggered only a short flurry of subsequent publications in the field of New Testament studies.[9] But as John Gager shows in this volume through his examination of the work of Girard's disciple, Robert Hamerton-Kelly, such a line of thinking has the potential to reinscribe insidiously the prejudices of Marcion.

In spite of these general trends, there have been scattered studies of violence in the New Testament. An early and classic study was Douglas Hare's work on persecution in the Gospel of Matthew with his careful exegesis and analysis of Matthew's redactional layers serving as an important caution against naïve readings of New Testament passages concerning violence.[10] In the past decade both Richard Horsley and Warren Carter have brought consideration of the violence of the Roman Empire from the margins to the center of New Testament studies in their work on Paul, Jesus, and the Gospel of Matthew.[11] Jennifer Glancy's recent work, *Slavery in Early Christianity,* has brought into focus the heretofore largely ignored question of the violence directed against slaves in emerging Christianity, drawing evidence from even the earliest layers of the Jesus tradition.[12] The most comprehensive treatment to date, however, is Michel Desjardins's *Peace, Violence, and the New Testament.*[13] Resisting the trend to emphasize the preaching of love and peace and to overlook the passages that recount or authorize violence, Desjardins provides even attention to both. As Desjardins himself confesses, however, this book, aimed at a general audience, is not likely to satisfy the historical-critical scholar. Instead of placing individual documents in their specific historical contexts, Desjardins defers to the texts as a canonical collection and reaches for a synthetic and comprehensive statement on the New Testament's position on violence.

We take a new tack in this volume, bringing together six studies prepared in connection with a Society of Biblical Literature special session on violence among Jews and Christians. They focus on violence in these specific textual complexes: the writings of Paul, the Q document,

texts related most directly to historical Jesus study; the Gospels of
Matthew and John; and the book of Acts. Contributors to this volume
consider a broad range of violent depictions and exhortations, including
pronouncements that God condemns nonbelievers to a fiery hell, accounts
of Jesus engaged in battle with demons, and Paul's desire to castrate his
Galatian opponents.

Of special interest in several of these articles are the depictions of violence among followers of Jesus and other Jews, and the implications of
these depictions for subsequent relationships between communities of
Jews and Christians. Indeed, a major impetus for this collection is our
concern to think more rigorously about how to read these depictions of
violence in the community formation of Jesus followers. We raise questions of the relationship of text to reality, of narrative to history, in the
face of the embedded memories of Christian innocence and Jewish culpability forged on the multiple New Testament depictions of Jesus and his
followers as victims of violence, and other Jews as agents of that violence.[14] While some important progress on these issues has been made
as a result of the intense scrutiny of Jewish agency in the death of Jesus,
the same scrutiny is surprisingly absent from treatments of violence
among other Jews in the New Testament. Following Elizabeth Castelli's
observation that "historical criticism of ancient religious texts can be read
as resistance to the predominance of memory as a governing value in
those texts,"[15] we observe that current scholarly resistance to the cultural
memory of Jews as Christ killers[16] is matched by acquiescence to the governing memory of Jews as killing Christ's followers. That is, while the
rhetorical and ideological forces now recognized as motivating gospel
authors to spotlight Jewish culpability in Jesus' death make it impossible
for modern scholars to read the passion accounts as windows onto historical events, accounts of Jewish violence against Jesus followers are generally accepted as factually reliable. To point out but one striking instance of
this phenomenon, it is virtually impossible to find a scholarly treatment of
the stoning of Stephen at the hands of a Jewish mob that does not start
from the premise of this incident's historicity.[17]

While this volume situates itself generally within studies of violence
and religion, its special focus is on violent language about, and depictions
of violent incidents among, Jews in the New Testament. Here we build
upon the studies of anti-Judaic language in early Christianity, including
for instance, those that have developed Georg Simmel's insight that the
most intense form of conflict is that between intimate enemies.[18] Students

of Simmel began to see anti-Jewish vitriol not as a sign of conflict between two well-formed religious entities but as the product of the process of separation between intimately related groups trying to construct independent identities. On this model, much of the violent rhetoric attributed to Jesus in the Gospels is read as more indicative of violent separation in post-crucifixion community formation than of Jesus' actual hostility toward fellow Jews. As Judith Lieu has aptly summarized this approach, albeit with an eye to the second century, "Gospel authors also tell the story of Jesus in the light of their own experience, and . . . on their pages, Jesus' encounters with *his* contemporaries reflect more than a little about the early Christians' own encounters with theirs."[19] J. Louis Martyn's theory about the expulsion passages in John, however much debated in its particulars, still contains the now widely recognized insight that the author told at least two stories at once, one about the time of Jesus and one about his own community's experience of rejection.[20] These redactional insights eventually led to sociological analysis. In a now classic essay, Seán Freyne argued that "both Matthew's and John's vilification of the Jews comes directly and immediately from their concerns to define the identities of the communities for whom they wrote."[21] Several articles in this collection build on this foundation.

In many of these articles, Roman imperial violence, whose traces are often perceived only at the margins of New Testament texts, emerges as the overarching framework in which these biblical texts are written. The violence of colonizer over colonized and the subsequent inward turn of violence among the colonized are exposed in canonical gospel, Apocalypse, and Acts. Thus, texts that have often been read solely in terms of ethnic and religious conflict between Jews and Christians are further nuanced by questions of political dynamics, of elite leaders' complicity with the occupying power, and of internalized communal blame among the occupied in face of the occupier's violence. As Melanie Johnson-DeBaufre discusses by way of an analogy between Roman-occupied Judea and English-occupied Antigua, the narrative world of early Jesus followers may lie "far from the metropolitan center that rules," but its rhetoric is nevertheless informed by that center. Close attention to the relationship between Roman center and Judean periphery helps to clarify the purposes and effects of that rhetoric.

To question historicity of these depictions or to embed them in their larger imperial context is not to suggest that Jews never inflicted violence upon followers of Jesus. In the ancient world, as in our own, religious conflict can and will occasionally rise to this level. And of course, Paul's letters confirm that Jews and Jesus followers were no exception. The interpretive strategies described above, however, help us to avoid pitfalls common to this discussion. All the contributors acknowledge a debt to rhetorical analyses of the New Testament in the language they use to describe Jesus and his followers. Avoiding the term Christian, a variety of alternatives are employed in this endeavor: Jesus followers, Jesus believers, Jews devoted to Jesus. But this is not merely a picayune matter of chronological consistency resulting from the fact that our authors write for the most part about times and texts that predate the first occurrences of the word "Christian." Rather it is an essential signal of our and their engagement in a much broader debate about the timing and nature of the partings of the ways.[22] Such care underlines the complex and extended process that ultimately transformed Jesus followers from a Jewish sect into a distinct religious entity and attempts to foreclose the domineering cultural impulse of Christian triumphalism that in this context results in juxtaposing Jew/violent/persecutor with Christian/peaceful/innocent.

John Gager, with Leigh Gibson, begins by calling into question the assumption that the Apostle Paul's violence owes to a predilection of first-century Judaism. Situating their argument against that of Robert Hamerton-Kelly, a Girardian disciple who does explain Paul's violence as the expression of a typical first-century Jew, Gager instead locates an explanation in Paul's peculiar personality and idiosyncratic ideology. Building on recent scholarship on Paul, Gager critiques many of the assumptions on which Hamerton-Kelly's Pauline portrait is based, including the notion that Judaism turned the law into a weapon of exclusion as regards the Gentiles. Instead Gager offers a selection of Pauline passages that illustrate how a rhetoric of violence infuses the core of Pauline writings, pointing out that in Paul's decision to make the cross the centerpiece of his Christology he has embraced the most "violent symbol in the entire Mediterranean world."

Melanie Johnson-DeBaufre's article tackles the *Sophia* predictions of violence in Q 11:39–48 in which "this generation" is held responsible for previous killings and persecutions of prophets. Drawing on earlier scholarship that pointed to the intra-Jewish dimensions of these accusations, Johnson-DeBaufre probes further to analyze the motif's origin in the Hebrew Bible where, she argues, it is invoked to illustrate how Israel's missteps have lead to national suffering. In turn, Johnson-DeBaufre posits that the Q community imported this same motif into a first-century-C.E.

context: the rhetoric of communal blame was used to explain the suffering that accompanied the Jewish War. Ultimately the Hebrew Bible's killing of the prophets motif would be lost as later gospel authors recast it as a statement of Jewish responsibility for Jesus' death in order to script Jesus more convincingly as a prophet martyred by his own people.

John Marshall's chapter on the Apocalypse of John applies some of his provocative insights about the text specifically to the issue of violence.[23] Key to Marshall's work on the Apocalypse is his conviction that the text dates to the Jewish War and some elements reflect an intra-Jewish dispute—insights that quickly recast how one views the violence in the text. If the text dates to the Jewish War, for instance, the violence in the text falls into two categories, neither of which sustains the common reading of Revelation as evincing conflict between Jews and Christians. On the one hand, the text attempts to rewrite the impending victory of Rome (figured as Babylon) over Jerusalem and their respective divine protectors, Satan and the God of Israel. On the other hand, it serves as an intra-Jewish diatribe directed at Jezebel, who represents Jews who commingle too freely with the Gentile world. In the final stage of the paper, postcolonial theory is invoked to demonstrate how the latter, the intra-group conflict, can be understood as an offshoot of the former, colonial domination.

Where John Marshall's contribution culminates in a discussion of the rich perspective that postcolonial theory can bring to the Apocalypse of John, Richard Horsley's treatment of Jesus and imperial violence incorporates the insights of postcolonial reflection from the outset. Jesus, Horsley argues, has long been cast as a teacher of love as opposed to a resistance fighter, a characterization consonant with the origins of modern New Testament studies in the heyday of European imperialism, but overdue for reconsideration. Working from a growing consensus that Jews enjoyed no exemption from "brutal military violence against subject people" that was standard Roman practice, Horsley locates Jesus within the spectrum of resistance movements. Working from Mark and Q, the earliest sources about Jesus, he pursues three lines of argument. First, Horsley connects Jesus' exorcisms to the larger issue of imperial resistance, crowning this section with an insightful exposition of Jesus' expulsion of Legion from the demoniac. Second, Horsley reexamines Jesus' calls for love of one's neighbor in the context of Jesus' engagement with, not separation from, Jewish resistance to Rome. Third, Horsley returns to Jesus' expectation of God's judgment and the violence it entails, challenging previous generations of scholars who have tried to drain these predictions of their connection to violent action.

Warren Carter, like Richard Horsley, puts imperial violence front and center in his analysis of the identities of agents of violence in the Gospel of Matthew. Carter argues that class and status, rather than ethnicity, are the key factors in Matthew's constructions of violence. After considering definitions of violence ranging from those restricted to the immediate exercise of physical force to wider definitions that take structural/systemic and societal dimensions into account, Carter concludes that elite groups are the dominant agents of violence in Matthew. This elite cannot be subdivided into Gentile and Jew, but is composed of "an alliance of Gentiles (kings, governors, Pilate) and Jews (the Jerusalem elite: chief priests, Pharisees and scribes, synagogue authorities, etc.)." Though the social and political elite are responsible for most of the violence in Matthew, Carter observes that Matthew has situated this violence within a larger cosmic frame, in which violent eschatological consequences threaten the elite. Through these violent visions of God's eschatological triumph, Carter concludes, "Matthew's gospel finally, but ironically, capitulates to and imitates the imperial violence from which it seeks to save."

Two articles in this collection examine the plausibility and representation of violence against Christians. Both Adele Reinhartz (Gospel of John) and Shelly Matthews (Acts of the Apostles) avoid the claim that Jews never acted against Christians. Nonetheless they suggest that the actions alleged in these two texts lack historical plausibility, and therefore invite reinterpretation, not as descriptions of events that occurred but as attempts to prescribe how Jews and Christians should be understood. Using a grammatical metaphor, Reinhartz seeks to parse at three textual levels the relationship between the Gospel of John's commandment to love and its depictions of Jewish violent intentions and acts: the historical level, the level of the Johannine community (ecclesiological), and finally, the cosmological level. On each of these levels, the perpetrators and victims of violence shift. On the historical and ecclesiological levels, the Jews perpetrate violence respectively against Jesus and his followers. On the cosmological level, there is a reversal: God punishes Jews for their actions and revokes his covenant with them. Invoking the tight and sometimes causal relationships among each level's grammar of violence, Reinhartz worries about the continuing appeal that a long-standing theory of J. L. Martyn continues to hold for many scholars. While Martyn argued that the three expulsion texts in the Gospel of John reflect a reality of the

Johannine community itself, Reinhartz suggests that the cosmological tale drives the narrative and grammar of violence on the other two levels.

Like Reinhartz, Matthews is reluctant to see allegations of violent behavior as direct windows onto historical violence. Her argument begins by demonstrating how the death of Stephen yokes the death of Jesus and the narrative of Paul, creating an interpenetrating, and thus tightly bound, narrative. Matthews finds in Stephen's carefully crafted speech too neat a critique of ritual for a first-century Jesus follower, and suggests that the historical-sounding Stephen story has hoodwinked too many of its interpreters. This verdict, however, does not reduce the story's value as a resource in understanding the early Jesus movement, but rather opens up new vistas for investigation. Here Matthews's piece intersects with the other major theme in this collection: imperial power. By way of an overture to Roman authority, Luke seeks to depict Jews and Jewish legal processes in a negative light and this tendency governs his account of Stephen's death. In contrast to depictions of both Roman and Jewish involvement in the crucifixion of Jesus and the imprisonment of Paul, Jews alone drive the judicial proceeding against Stephen, which results in the exclusively Jewish punishment of stoning.

The general issue of violence among Jews and Christians, and in the case of this volume, the specific instances that are recorded in the New Testament anthology, justify greater consideration on the grounds of the question's own intrinsic merit but also because of the long shadow these accounts have cast on Western history. In comparing the treatment of Jews in Christian and Muslim societies, Mark Cohen comments on the effect stories of Jewish violence against early Christians had: "Exaggerated or not, an indelible memory of Jewish persecution of Christians became embedded in Christian consciousness. This memory ... would later nourish irrational fantasies about Jewish violence toward Christians, invoked to justify a militant Christian response, both verbal and physical, to Judaism and the Jews."[24] Were it only the case that such thinking were limited to medieval or pre-Nazi Europe!

Writing this introduction in the spring of 2004, in the wake of the release of Mel Gibson's movie, *The Passion of the Christ,* we could not be more aware of the tenacity of this memory. In the weeks following the release of the film, the Pew Research Center for the People and the Press conducted a survey that included consideration of whether viewing *The Passion of the Christ* increased belief that Jews were responsible for Jesus' death.[25] In spite of a wide consensus among scholars of the New

Testament to the contrary, a view that received wide media coverage prior to the poll, the percentage of Americans who hold that Jews are responsible for the death of Jesus has increased (up overall to 26 percent from 19 percent in a 1997 ABC News poll), with an even steeper increase among people under thirty (21 to 42 percent). Clearly there remains a great need for scholarly engagement with these issues and for their work to find a wider audience. We offer these studies in hopes of facilitating such engagement.

Notes

1. Marcion's anti-Jewishness was wide in scope, extending beyond his relatively well-known distinction between New and Old Testament Gods and into his soteriology. According to Irenaeus (*Haer.* 1.27.3), Marcion taught that on Christ's descent into the underworld, he redeemed the likes of Cain, the Sodomites, the Egyptians, and all the maligned Gentiles everywhere. Only those associated with the Jewish God—including the righteous patriarchs and prophets—were beyond redemption by the God of mercy and love.

2. René Girard, *Violence and the Sacred* (trans. Patrick Gregory; Baltimore: Johns Hopkins University Press, 1972).

3. Robert Orsi, "Snakes Alive: Resituating the Moral in the Study of Religion," in *In Face of the Facts: Moral Inquiry in American Scholarship* (ed. Richard Wightman Fox and Robert B. Westbrook; Woodrow Wilson Center Series; Cambridge: Cambridge University Press, 1998), 201–26.

4. Elizabeth Castelli, *Martyrdom and Memory: Early Christian Culture Making* (New York: Columbia University Press, 2004).

5. Regina Schwartz, *The Curse of Cain: The Violent Legacy of Monotheism* (Chicago: University of Chicago Press, 1997).

6. Vivienne Jabri, "The Construction of Identity and the Discourse of Violence," in *Discourses on Violence: Conflict Analysis Reconsidered* (Manchester: Manchester University Press, 1996), 119–44.

7. *Religious Studies News/SBL Edition,* The Society of Biblical Literature, 4, no. 6 (June 2003).

8. René Girard, *Violence and the Sacred* (trans. Patrick Gregory; Baltimore: Johns Hopkins University Press, 1972), and idem, *Things Hidden Since the Foundation of the World* (trans. Stephen Bann and Michael Meteer; Stanford, Calif.: Stanford University Press, 1987). For a sympathetic but not uncritical summary of Girard on Christianity, see Lucien Scubla, "The Christianity of René Girard," in *Violence and Truth: On the Work of René Girard* (trans. Mark R. Anspach; Stanford, Calif.: Stanford University Press, 1988), 160–77.

9. Robert Hamerton-Kelly, *Sacred Violence: Paul's Hermeneutic of the Cross* (Minneapolis: Fortress Press, 1991); and James Williams, *The Bible, Violence, and the Sacred:*

Liberation from the Myth of Sanctioned Violence (San Francisco: HarperSanFrancisco, 1991).

10. Douglas R. A. Hare, *The Theme of Jewish Persecution of Christians in the Gospel According to St. Matthew* (Cambridge: Cambridge University Press, 1967), 80–96.

11. See the three volumes edited by Richard A. Horsley: *Paul and Empire: Religion and Power in Roman Imperial Society* (Harrisburg, Pa.: Trinity Press International, 1997); *Paul and Politics: Ekklesia, Israel, Imperium, Interpretation, Essays in Honor of Krister Stendahl* (Harrisburg, Pa.: Trinity Press International, 2000); *Jesus and Empire: The Kingdom of God and the New World Disorder* (Minneapolis: Fortress Press, 2003); and the studies of Warren Carter, *Matthew and the Margins: A Socio-political and Religious Reading* (Sheffield: Sheffield Academic Press, 2000); *Matthew and Empire: Initial Explorations* (Harrisburg, Pa.: Trinity Press International, 2001).

12. Jennifer A. Glancy, *Slavery in Early Christianity* (Oxford: Oxford University Press, 2002).

13. Michel Desjardin, *Peace, Violence, and the New Testament* (Sheffield: Sheffield Academic Press, 1997).

14. On questions of the relationship of rhetoric to reality in New Testament documents, and of the ethics of historical reconstruction of early Christianity, see Elisabeth Schüssler Fiorenza, *Rhetoric and Ethic: The Politics of Biblical Studies* (Minneapolis: Fortress Press, 1999).

15. Castelli, *Martyrdom and Memory*, 24.

16. Reexamination of the accuracy of the depictions of Jesus' crucifixion began almost two centuries ago in what James Parkes dubbed "the literature of defense," that is, the works of Jewish scholars calling into question the New Testament's depiction of Jews (James Parkes, *The Conflict of the Church and Synagogue* [London: Soncino Press, 1934; New York: Atheneum, 1985], xv). These works would have a halting impact on New Testament studies until the middle of the twentieth century. Among the many studies of these issues in the past decade are John Dominic Crossan, *Who Killed Jesus?* (San Francisco: HarperSanFrancisco, 1996); Elisabeth Schüssler Fiorenza, *Jesus: Miriam's Child, Sophia's Prophet* (New York: Continuum, 1994), 67-96; Ellis Rivkin, *What Crucified Jesus?: Messianism, Pharisaism, and the Development of Christianity* (New York: UAHC Press, 1997); James Carroll, *Constantine's Sword: The Church and the Jews* (Boston: Houghton Mifflin, 2001).

17. Todd Penner's important monograph, *In Praise of Christian Origins: Stephen and the Hellenists in Lukan Apologetic Historiography* (New York: T&T Clark International, 2004) has now become an exception in this regard. Unfortunately, his work appeared too late to be fully considered here. Perhaps a partial and elementary explanation for the state of scholarship on this issue stems from the nature of our sources. Historical-critical scholars have always had at the starting point of their Jesus research a multi-gospel canon. This kaleidoscope of Jesus portraits has served as open invitation to bring one historical portrait into focus and to necessarily relegate aspects of the Jesus story to the realm of the mythic. However, there is only one canonical (hi)story of the post-crucifixion development of the church of Jesus followers, the book of Acts. We do

not mean to suggest that we are unaware of how scholars, since the time of F. C. Baur and the Tübingen school, have applied critical approaches to the Acts narrative as well as to the Gospels. We note only that the univocity of this story—Luke's powerful authorial assurance that he provides for his readers' surety (*asphaleia*) in his "orderly account"—does not invite the same sort of parsing as a multiform story does.

18. Georg Simmel, *Conflict and the Web of Group-Affiliations* (trans. Kurt H. Wolff and Reinhard Bendix; New York: Free Press, 1955). Simmel's work appears in New Testament scholarship as early as the 1970s: see John G. Gager, *Kingdom and Community: The Social World of Early Christianity* (Englewood Cliffs, N.J.: Prentice Hall, 1975), 80.

19. Judith Lieu, *Image and Reality: The Jews in the World of the Christians in the Second Century* (Edinburgh: T&T Clark, 1996), 3.

20. J. Louis Martyn, *History and Theology in the Fourth Gospel* (3d ed.; New York: Harper & Row, 1968; Louisville, Ky.: Westminster John Knox, 2003).

21. Seán Freyne, "Vilifying the Other and Defining the Self: Matthew's and John's Anti-Jewish Polemic in Focus," in *"To See Ourselves as Others See Us": Christians, Jews, and "Others" in Late Antiquity* (ed. Jacob Neusner and Ernest S. Frerichs; Chico, Calif.: Scholars Press, 1985), 119.

22. An excellent overview of the ever changing thinking on the parting of the ways is now available in the introduction to Annette Yoshiko Reed and Adam H. Becker, eds., *The Ways That Never Parted: Jews and Christians in Late Antiquity and the Early Middle Ages* (Texts and Studies in Ancient Judaism; Tübingen: Mohr-Siebeck, 2003).

23. For a full discussion of his views, see John Marshall, *Parables of War: Reading John's Jewish Apocalypse* (Studies in Christianity and Judaism; Waterloo, Ont.: Wilfrid Laurier University Press, 2001).

24. Mark Cohen, "Jews in Christendom and Islam," in *Religious Violence between Christians and Jews: Medieval Roots, Modern Perspectives* (New York: Palgrave, 2002) 112.

25. "Belief That Jews Were Responsible for Christ's Death Increases; Prevalent Among Young People, Minorities, and 'Passion of Christ' Viewers," http://people-press.org/reports/display.php3?ReportID=209.

1

Violent Acts and Violent Language
in the Apostle Paul

JOHN G. GAGER, WITH E. LEIGH GIBSON

When we think of violence in the early centuries of the Common Era, our first instinct is to turn our eyes toward Rome.[1] Here was violence on a massive scale—ranging from the brutal spectacle of public games to the gruesome displays of public crucifixions. Public crucifixion in particular represented a form of state violence that served not only to punish miscreants of all sorts but also to warn others of Rome's readiness to deal with dissent by the systematic application of arbitrary measures cloaked in the garb of a judicial process.[2] When we think of violence among Jews in the period, whether in deed, language, or ideology, we have learned to focus on small fringe groups—Josephus's "bandits" in Galilee before the Jewish War of 66–70 C.E. and the infamous *sicarii* who carried out political assassinations of fellow Jews in the run-up to the same revolt. As for those mistakenly called Christians—Jesus, Paul, the authors of the Gospels of Matthew, Mark, and John—the image here goes in hand with the view that Christianity transcends Judaism in every arena, including the attitude toward violence. Nowhere is this pattern of thought more apparent than in the thought of the one highly influential figure who has drawn our attention to questions of violence—the French thinker René Girard.[3] For Girard, it is not just that Jesus advocates turning the other cheek and a total abnegation of violence in any form. Beyond that, his crucifixion as the innocent and wrongly accused victim reveals the mendacity of all forms of scapegoatism and sacrifice. In Jesus' violent death, we are all finally released from the vicious cycle of murderous rivalry, deformed desire, and the false foundations on which all subsequent societies have been constructed.

13

Paul presents a rather different case. And it is perhaps not surprising that Girard has little to say about him, as Paul does not clearly reflect the turn-the-other-cheek values that Girard so admires in Jesus. Indeed, it is well known that Paul's first contacts with the followers of Jesus were as their persecutor. Thus Paul is initially fully implicated in the cycle of sacred violence. The challenging task of integrating Paul into Girard's theory has fallen to his American disciple Robert Hamerton-Kelly in his *Sacred Violence: Paul's Hermeneutic of the Cross*.[4] Since my own thinking about Paul and violence has been shaped by my reading of Hamerton-Kelly, let me briefly summarize his views.

Following Girard's general theory of the origins of religion and society, Hamerton-Kelly places sacred violence at the heart of all religions, including Judaism. Thus Paul, as a Jew, was complicit in this cycle of violence, participating in the tradition of Jewish persecution of Judaism's own prophets through his persecution of the early Jesus believers. Only after his visionary experience could Paul move outside this tradition and recognize how the crucifixion of an innocent man lays bare the destructive cycle of sacred violence (60). Thus for Hamerton-Kelly, the Bible, and especially the cross, through their victim-centered stories, unleash "the unprecedented and unparalleled progress of Western civilization away from ritual and myth" and toward an ethic of love and nonviolence (38).

Hamerton-Kelly is well aware of the possible anti-Semitic elaborations of his view of Paul and works diligently (but with mixed success) against such an interpretation. For instance, in the case of Jesus' crucifixion, he is careful to acknowledge the historical responsibility of both Jews and Romans, and to extend theological responsibility for the act to the entire human race (64–65). And he holds that Paul strives to preserve the continuing value of the law/Torah, albeit at the expense of the Jews, who distorted it (140). On the other side, Judaism is presented as "a system of sacred violence in which sin misuses the Law as a part of its strategy to dominate all humanity" (108). But at the end, Hamerton-Kelly concludes, Paul was unable to break fully from Judaism. In what he calls a case of "nostalgia overwhelming his judgment," Hamerton-Kelly holds that Paul fractured but did not break his bonds with "the coils of sacred violence" (11).

I have no desire to turn this brief exercise into a full-blown critique of either Girard or Hamerton-Kelly. But since they are the major players in the field of violence and Paul, I cannot forego making a few passing remarks. First, it is worth noting that theological interests are paramount for both men.[5] Second, in Girard's case, the mix of Durkheim and Freud, with a heavy dose of continental phenomenology and Christian theology, suffers, like all such undertakings, from making global generalizations that tend to obliterate individual cases. At the same time, I do find Girard's treatment of distorted desire, and what he calls mimetic rivalry as sources of scapegoatism, to be an interesting and potentially fruitful way of looking at the deeper sources and forms of violence. There is clearly some relationship between thwarted or disguised desire and intense rivalry on the one hand and the impulse toward violence on the other.

But for me the bottom line is that Hamerton-Kelly's image of Paul, and sometimes of the New Testament as a whole, seems woefully out of date. Let me just cite some of the more salient examples in his interpretation that have been significantly attacked and widely revised: his reading of Rom 7 as an autobiographical text, challenged by W. G. Kümmel in 1929[6] and now rendered entirely implausible in the wake of Stanley Stowers's *A Rereading of Romans*;[7] his assumption that Paul's phrase "works of the law" means the Jewish way of life, which ignores the work of Lloyd Gaston[8] and others on the phrase; his view that Paul, in the end, locates the salvation of Israel in its acceptance of Christianity; his refusal to recognize the anti-Judaism or even the potential for it in the Gospels; his unquestioned use of the term "Christian" of Paul and his congregants; his notion that Judaism in general and Paul in particular turned the law into a weapon of exclusion and violence (here he places heavy emphasis on the problematic text in 1 Thess 2:14–15, long regarded as a later interpolation); and finally, his view that for Paul, and seemingly for Hamerton-Kelly too, the underlying focus of Judaism was the exclusion of Gentiles from the Jewish community.

Today none of these positions is recognizable as Pauline or Jewish. As I have argued elsewhere to an increasingly receptive audience, long-standing interpretations of Paul are plagued by at least three fatal missteps: a retrojection of later forms of Christian belief onto Paul; inaccurate identification of Paul's literary audience in the letters; and a profound ignorance and misunderstanding of Second Temple Judaism.[9] Simply put, we must learn to read Paul in his own time and place. We know, for example, that he shared with many Jews of the first century intense eschatological expectations and we must remain mindful of how deeply these expectations shaped his thoughts and actions from start to finish. Moreover, Krister Stendahl's landmark article about the dangers of modernizing Paul, particularly about the danger of reading Paul "in light of Luther's struggle with his conscience," remains as powerful today as when it was first published in 1963.[10] We also know, though we sometimes forget, that Paul understood himself, as the apostle to the Gentiles, to be engaged in a mission to a Gentile audience (Rom 11:13, 15:16; Gal 1:16, 2:2, etc.). There is simply no evidence that he ever deviated from this focus. Furthermore, his interest in the Gentiles and in the possibility of their salvation at the end of time, namely, his time, cannot be understood as a view that places him outside of Judaism: no Jew, with the possible exception of radical sectarians like the Qumranites, held such a view.[11] And it was certainly not characteristic of the Pharisees, to whom Paul professed allegiance (see Matt 23:15: "Woe to you Pharisees, hypocrites. For you cross sea and land to make a single proselyte [= convert].")

Even working with these simple caveats, the traditional interpretation of Paul as breaking with his Jewish heritage, addressing audiences of both Jews and Gentiles, and rejecting the ongoing validity of Torah for Jews simply cannot be maintained. Instead, I have argued alongside Lloyd Gaston, numerous Jewish interpreters of Paul,[12] and an ever growing number of other scholars that Paul advanced a novel view on the relationship between Gentiles, Jews, and God, a view that has been widely misunderstood from the start. With the eschaton at hand, Paul believed that God had sent Jesus to fulfill an important, yet still outstanding promise: that the children of Abraham would become a great nation. The descendants of Jacob (Israel) had long since accepted Torah, but Gentiles, also children of Abraham, were still unaccounted for in salvation history. Now, at the end of history, Jesus had been sent to them. For Gentiles alone, Torah was no longer the path to salvation; for Jews, observance of Torah remained essential. Thus, when Paul speaks negatively in his letters about the law, he addresses those Gentile Jesus believers who have taken upon themselves, under pressure from other apostles within the Jesus movement, a limited range of Torah observances.

In spite of the deep divide between Hamerton-Kelly's and my own interpretations of Paul, his *Sacred Violence* is useful for setting out my own views on Paul and violence. Unlike Hamerton-Kelly, I reject the view that Paul's violence is to be understood and explained as a simple consequence of the fact that he was a Jew; unlike Hamerton-Kelly, I see Paul not as a typical Jew, but rather, in his own words, as eccentric precisely in his attraction to violence; unlike Hamerton-Kelly, I see the post-conversion Paul as still very much entangled in the coils of violence; unlike Hamerton-Kelly, in the end, I see Paul as a violent *personality,* in his actions, in his language, and in his ideology of Gentiles and their world as a world of violence.

First, a word about Paul's preconversion persecution of Jesus follow-ers, which certainly qualifies as an act or, better, as series of acts of vio-lence. Though some apologetic interpreters have attempted to play down these acts, Paul's own language—and thus his perception of the acts them-selves—is anything but moderate. In Phil 3:6 he describes himself as a per-secutor of the community. In Gal 1:13 he elaborates: he persecuted the community of God violently and sought to annihilate it. What served as the specific occasion for his murderous violence we will never know for certain, although my own best guess is that it must have had something to do with his sense that Gentiles were being allowed into the community of Israel in a way that threatened his sense of Israel's integrity.[13]

Second, we know of no other identifiable figures who, like Paul, devoted themselves to persecuting the followers of Jesus. What is more, in the very same passage where Paul proclaims that he sought to destroy the community, he goes out of his way to present himself as an over-the-top Jew among his peers—"I advanced in Judaism beyond many of my own age, so extremely zealous for the traditions of my fathers" (Gal 1:14). In other words, Paul strives to distance himself from other Jews on precisely this issue: he was exceptional rather than typical. My prelimi-nary view is thus that Paul's violence was not the inevitable result of the mere fact that he was a Jew (Hamerton-Kelly's position), but that his per-sonality and his eccentric ideology were factors that drew him to those traditions within ancient Judaism that gave outlet and support to his pri-or inclinations.

Third, with this preliminary result in mind, I turn next to look at Paul's use of violent language, on the theory that violence is not just a matter of acts (the "walk," if you will) but also a matter of words (the "talk"). Here I was reminded of a lesson that my parents tried to teach me when I was young—one of the many lessons that it took me years to unlearn: "Sticks and stones can break my bones, but words will never hurt me." But vio-lent words do hurt—by themselves and as precursors to violent acts. And what I found as I reread Paul's letters from this perspective came as some-thing of a revelation. What follows is a selection, by no means complete, meant to illustrate how a rhetoric of violence infuses the very core of Paul's writings.

God, as is commonly the case in eschatologically preoccupied texts (see, for example, the book of Revelation in the New Testament and the *War Scroll* from Qumran), is a violent actor, inflicting his wrath on the unrighteous. Paul is no exception in this respect. The final culmination of history will be violent and will witness widespread destruction and suffering (1 Thess 5:3). Nor are those to be punished distant outsiders. Even Paul's opponents within the Jesus movement receive repeated warnings of imminent destruction:

- "[do not be] frightened by your opponents. This is a clear omen to them of their destruction . . . and that from God (Phil 1:28);
- ". . . there will be wrath and fury . . . tribulation and distress for everyone who does evil" (2 Cor 2:8).

Nor is such violent action reserved for God alone. Paul believes that he too is entitled (as an agent of God?) to act specifically against those who stand in opposition to his gospel. It may even be that he feels entitled to act in this manner because he believes that his violent action is a rightful part of the End that has already begun to unfold.

- "If we or even an angel from heaven should preach a gospel contrary to what we preached to you, let him be accursed" (Gal 1:8) and again "Let him be cursed" (1:9).
- "I wish that those who are disturbing you would castrate [or worse] themselves" (Gal 5:12).
- "Look out for the dogs . . . the mutilators of the flesh" (Phil 3:2).
- "You are to deliver this man [a member of the community in Corinth] over to Satan for the destruction of his flesh" (1 Cor 5:5).

In an ironic yet familiar twist, Pauline violence targets not only the unrighteous and wicked but also the righteous. For Paul, violence and suffering serve as markers of authentic apostleship. He regularly commends those followers who have undergone tribulation for the sake of their communities. Indeed, the more violence endured, the greater the individual's status within the movement. To this end, Paul twice boasts extravagantly in defending himself and his apostolic credentials before his Corinthian audience.[14] Characterizing himself and his colleagues, he boasts that they/we have "commended ourselves in every way: through great endurances, hardships, calamities, beatings, imprisonments, riots, labors" (2 Cor 6:5; compare a similar list of miseries in 11:23–29). But it was not enough simply to have suffered violence. The closer the apostle himself came to violent death, the more his message reflected this fervent conviction.[15]

- "As it is written, 'For your sake we are being killed all day long; we are counted as sheep to be slaughtered'" (Rom 8:36, quoting Ps 44:22).
- "For I think that God has exhibited us apostles as last of all, as though sentenced to death . . ." (1 Cor 4:9).

Paul, however, found the ultimate proof of authentic apostleship in crucifixion. Although actual crucifixion was surely unlikely for members of the Pauline communities, the idea of crucifixion is held up repeatedly as a metaphor for the transformative process that marked the discipleship of Jesus. In Gal 2:19, where Paul recounts the Jerusalem gathering and reminds his readers of the endorsement he had received there, he makes a bold claim: "I have been co-crucified with Christ." And in Rom 6:6, this time speaking in the plural, he repeats the claim: "We know that our old self was crucified with him so that the body of sin might be destroyed. . . ."

In conclusion, I would offer two brief observations about what I have called this Pauline penchant for violent language. The first is that a good deal of what I have called Paul's violent language, especially about himself and his sufferings, must be seen as theological, or better, christological. There is no more violent symbol in the entire Mediterranean world than that of crucifixion. And Paul's stance here is unmistakable: "I was determined not to know anything with you except Jesus Christ and him crucified" (1 Cor 2:2). From this follows all of Paul's talk about his own sufferings as well as those of his congregants. Suffering and participation in the violent act of crucifixion is his way of participating in Christ.

So far so good: we can agree, I think, that Paul's christological commitment to the crucified Christ accounts for much of his violent language. But here we must pause for a moment and, like good amateur psychologists, ask why it was that Paul was attracted to this particular christological package among the many that we know were available at the time—Jesus the prophet, Jesus the teacher, Jesus the healer, Jesus the gloriously resurrected Son of God in heaven, and others. In fact, it could well be argued that Paul's commitment to the crucified Christ was highly eccentric within the early Jesus movement, both before and after his time. But my real point here is that we need to consider the possibility that it was Paul's own personality, his own predilection for images and symbols of violence, in his own terms, his "excessive zeal," that led him to adopt and perhaps even to invent this violent Christology of the cross.[16]

Notes

1. The literature on the role of violence in Roman culture is extensive. I list but a few examples: Keith Hopkins, *Death and Renewal* (Sociological Studies in Roman History 2; Cambridge: Cambridge University Press, 1983); Michael B. Poliakoff, *Combat Sports in the Ancient World: Competition, Violence, and Culture* (New Haven, Conn.: Yale University Press, 1987); Magnus Wistrand, *Entertainment and Violence in Ancient Rome: The Attitudes of Roman Writers of the First Century A.D.* (Studia Graeca et Latina Gothoburgensia 56; Göteborg, Sweden: Acta Universitatis Gothoburgensis, 1992); Andrew Lintott, *Violence in Republican Rome* (2d ed.; Oxford: Oxford University Press, 1999).

2. See Martin Hengel, *Crucifixion in the Ancient World and the Folly of the Message of the Cross* (Philadelphia: Fortress Press, 1977).

3. As laid out in René Girard, *Violence and the Sacred* (trans. Patrick Gregory; Baltimore: Johns Hopkins University Press, 1972); and *Things Hidden Since the Foundation of the World* (trans. Stephen Bann and Michael Meteer; Stanford, Calif.: Stanford University Press, 1987).

4. Robert Hamerton-Kelly, *Sacred Violence: Paul's Hermeneutic of the Cross* (Minneapolis: Fortress Press, 1991).

5. For analyses of the theological dimensions of these authors, see John Dunhill, "Methodological Rivalries: Theology and Social Science in Girardian Interpretation of the New Testament," *JSNT* 62 (1996): 105–119; and Dale Martin, "Sacred Violence: Paul's Hermeneutic of the Cross," *Modern Theology* 9 (1993): 225–28.

6. Werner Georg Kümmel, *Römer 7 und das Bild des Menschen im Neuen Testament* (Leipzig: J. C. Hinrichs, 1929).

7. Stanley K. Stowers, *A Rereading of Romans: Justice, Jews, and Gentiles* (New Haven, Conn.: Yale University Press, 1994).

8. See Gaston's collected essays, *Paul and the Torah* (Vancouver: University of British Columbia Press, 1987).

9. John G. Gager, *Reinventing Paul: Israel and Gentiles in Paul's Gospel* (New York: Oxford University Press, 2000).

10. Krister Stendahl, "Paul and the Introspective Conscience of the West," *HTR* 56 (1963): 198–215. Reprinted in Krister Stendahl, *Paul among Jews and Gentiles, and Other Essays* (Philadelphia: Fortress Press, 1976), 78–96.

11. See the extensive list of Jewish texts in Terence L. Donaldson, *Paul and the Gentiles: Remapping the Apostle's Convictional World* (Minneapolis: Fortress Press, 1997), 51-81, where it becomes patently clear that for many Jews in the time of Paul a two-path view of salvation was the norm, with one path for Jews/Israel and and a different one for Gentiles.

12. See especially Michael Wyschogrod, "The Impact of Dialogue with Christianity on My Self-Understanding as a Jew," in *Die Hebräische Bibel und ihre zweifache Nachgeschichte: Festschrift für Rolf Rendtorffzum 65. Geburtstag* (ed. Blum von Erhard, Christian Macholz, and Ekkehard W. Stegemann; Neukirchen-Vluyn: Neukirchener Verlag, 1990), 725–36.

13. See the recent discussion by Justin Taylor, "Why Did Paul Persecute the Church?" in *Tolerance and Intolerance in Early Judaism and Christianity* (Cambridge: Cambridge University Press, 1998), 99–120.

14. For a recent treatment of this boasting of which I was not able to take account, see Jennifer A. Glancy, "Boasting of Beatings," *JBL* 123 (2004): 99–135.

15. For a treatment of the themes of violence and honor in the broader Roman world, see Carlin Barton, "Savage Miracles: The Redemption of Lost Honor in Roman Society and the Sacrament of the Gladiator and the Martyr," *Representations* 45 (1994): 41–71.

16. On the intriguing and much debated question of connections between Paul and the Gospel of Mark, see S. G. F. Brandon, *Jesus and the Zealots: A Study of the Political Factor in Primitive Christianity* (Manchester: Manchester University Press, 1967); and Joel Marcus, "Mark—Interpreter of Paul," *NTS* 46 (2000): 473–87.

2

The Blood Required of This Generation:
Interpreting Communal Blame in a Colonial Context*

MELANIE JOHNSON-DEBAUFRE

In *Culture and Imperialism,* Edward Said exposes the colonialist mapping of Jane Austen's *Mansfield Park.*[1] There are two estates in the novel—the English estate of Sir Thomas Bertram and his Antiguan estate to which he periodically travels. The England estate stands at the center of the novel's map: here the characters interact and the plot develops. The Antigua estate lurks at the periphery, referred to incidentally and in passing. No scenes are set there and no characters from that estate figure prominently in the novel. And yet the wealth generated by the Antigua estate—with its sugar cane crops and its slave labor—make the narrative world of *Mansfield Park* possible.[2] Characteristic of many postcolonial voices, Said points to the borderlands of Austen's narrative world and calls her readers to see how the center renders the periphery invisible even as its identity and story is inextricably interwoven with it.

The early Jesus tradition manifests a similar kind of mapping, but this time in reverse. In the Saying Source Q,[3] the periphery is at the center of the text because its narrative world lies far from the metropolitan center that rules the empire. The conflicts in the text encode tensions among Jews around issues of religious and social difference that sometimes culminate in the persecution and even killing of God's prophets. But as in *Mansfield Park,* the rhetoric of the text takes shape in the larger context of

* A shorter version of this essay was presented in the Consultation on Violence Among Jews and Christians held at the annual meeting of the American Academy of Religion and Society of Biblical Literature in Atlanta, Georgia, in November 2003. I thank Shelly Matthews, Leigh Gibson, and the panel participants for their helpful feedback and for the opportunity to participate in this important conversation.

22

empire, in this case, the first-century context of the Roman Empire.[4] Said's analysis of Austen raises a question: Does the situation of empire inform the rhetoric of Q in ways not often articulated or explored?

This essay explores this question by examining the judgment oracle in Q 11:49–51. In this passage, *Sophia*'s charge against "this generation" dramatically concludes a series of sayings in which Jesus accuses the leaders of the people of injustice and corruption (Q 11:39–48). "Therefore also *Sophia*[5] said: I will send them prophets and sages, and some of them they will kill and persecute, so that the blood of all the prophets poured out from the founding of the world may be required of this generation, from the blood of Abel to the blood of Zechariah, murdered between the sacrificial altar and the House. Yes, I tell you, it will be required of this generation" (49–51).[6] The oracle maps the recent behavior of the leaders onto a larger communal pattern of killing and persecuting God's prophets and then declares that "this generation" bears the guilt for the entire violent history of the rejection of God's message. How can we explain Q's rhetoric of communal blame? Why does the text move from a critique of corrupt leaders to imagining that *Sophia* will hold an entire generation responsible for "the blood of all the prophets poured out from the founding of the world"?

Scholars frequently present two explanations for such rhetoric either separately or in combination: (1) the Q community is trying to make sense of the violent death of Jesus at the hands of people in power;[7] or (2) the Q community is reacting to its own experiences of rejection and even persecution by other Jews.[8] Both arguments attempt to clarify the role that Q's announcement of communal judgment against "this generation" may have played in the formation of group identity within the larger group, "Israel." This is an important task because this Q text and others like it have a bloody history in the early Christian traditions about Jews as Christ-killers. Thus the effort to situate the polemics of the gospels in the context of internecine conflict *among* first-century Jews is valuable both historically and ethically. However, explicating these texts in their historical context cannot alone solve the problem of Christian anti-Judaism and anti-Semitism, nor should historical explanation be deployed as an apology for the polemic of the early Jesus tradition.[9] Understanding the context is one important strategy—alongside others—for recognizing and taking responsibility for the consequences of this kind of rhetoric.

In Q studies, however, locating polemical texts in the context of intra-Jewish debate can unwittingly result in a mistaken conclusion: all texts about communal blame and punishment stem from intra-Jewish conflict about identity or other issues. This approach unduly emphasizes the differences and tensions among various Jewish groups rather than the common concerns, traditions, and values of the larger group, "Israel." Said's identification of the incidental but crucial presence of the Antigua estate in *Mansfield Park* presses us to ask whether the realities of Roman imperial violence in first-century Judea lurking at the periphery of Q's rhetoric about communal blame and suffering exert more power on the center than we are accustomed to seeing.

Similar reflections on communal blame in the Israelite tradition emerge from other instances of national suffering, which produce crises of covenantal theology. For example, Jewish reflection on the death or rejection of the prophets appears routinely in discussions of the tragedy of exile or the destruction of the Second Temple at the end of the Jewish War. In addition, Jewish exegetical and haggadic traditions identify the murder of Zechariah (described in 2 Chr 24 and alluded to in Q 11:50) as a possible reason for the exile and an explanation for the suffering of either the Babylonian destruction of Jerusalem or the Roman destruction of Jerusalem. By placing Q 11:49–51 in this context, we can explore the emergence of communal blame as a response to Jewish suffering at the hands of Roman imperial power.

The Contours of Communal Blame and Communal Suffering in Q 11:49–51

The oracle against "this generation" concludes a series of woe-sayings in which Jesus criticizes the insufficient piety of Jewish leaders. The last woe in 11:47–48 introduces the theme of murdered prophets and presses the leaders to see that they are not different from their forefathers who killed the prophets: "Woe to you, for you build the tombs of the prophets, but your forefathers killed them. Thus you witness against yourselves that you are the sons of your forefathers."[10]

Even though the leaders set up memorials to God's prophets, their unwillingness to heed the message of the prophets—specified in the preceding series of woes—renders them children of their murderous forefathers.[11] Their present failings have been written into the whole history of Israel. In the following judgment oracle, *Sophia*—the wisdom of God—warns that this generation may have to pay for the blood of all the righteous ones and prophets of God spilled from the founding of the world.

This text characterizes communal blame and suffering in three ways. First, "this generation" bears the cumulative blame of earlier generations. It is the time of crisis when—so to speak—the sins of the fathers visit upon the sons. The illustrations of this disobedience span Israel's sacred history from Abel (Gen 4:1–12) to Zechariah (2 Chr 24:17–25). In both cases, the blood spilled through murder requires avenging. Abel's blood cries out from the ground (Gen 4:10) and Zechariah cries out before dying that he be avenged (2 Chr 24:22). These two murders typify the blood spilled whenever Israel rejected God's messengers or righteous ones.

Second, this generation will suffer physically and violently, paying with their own blood for the sins of all previous generations.[12] Thus the oracle prophesies that a *bloody* crisis awaits, a prediction Jesus confirms: "Yes, I tell you, it shall be required of this generation" (11:51). However, we are left to wonder by whom and how God's punishment will be exacted. A second *Sophia* oracle, Q 13:34–35, which follows Q 11:49–51 in Matthew, may provide the answer: "O Jerusalem, Jerusalem, who kills the prophets and stones those sent to her! How often I wanted to gather your children together, as a hen gathers her nestlings under her wings, but you were not willing! Look, your house is forsaken! I tell you, you will not see me until the time comes when you say: 'Blessed is the one who comes in the name of the Lord!'"[13] This oracle invokes the same history of the killing of the prophets, but this time, it is Jerusalem that has accrued guilt for killing the prophets and stoning those sent to her. And it is Jerusalem that suffers. *Sophia* mourns for Jerusalem like a mother whose children have refused her protection. This rejection results in Jerusalem's house being forsaken. The quotation from Ps 118:26 (LXX 117:26) suggests that the divine presence has left the temple in Jerusalem and will not return until the people turn again to welcome the messengers of God. Thus a third characteristic of communal blame and suffering may be that it is apparent in the destruction of Jerusalem and of the temple.[14]

Are the Q people staking a claim to true Judaism and thus announcing judgment on their opponents? Or do they explain the communal suffering of the Jewish War by invoking the traditions of Israel? The parallels with other Jewish uses of the motif of the death of the prophets point convincingly to the latter.

Jewish Reflections on Communal Blame and Suffering

I will discuss these Jewish reflections in three sections: (1) the motif of the rejection of the Law and the Prophets; (2) the murder of Zechariah; and (3) the biographies of the prophets.

Rejecting the Law and the Prophets

The motif of the violent death of the prophets appears in the Hebrew Scriptures less than scholars once thought. Following Odil Hannes Steck, Q scholars once understood the motif of the persecution of the prophets to be a central feature of a Deuteronomistic view of history.[15] Recently, however, it has become apparent that our understanding of Deuteronomistic theology needs revision. The motif of communal blame for the violent death of the prophets appears only in Neh 9:26, Jer 2:30, and 2 Chr 36:16.[16] In all three cases, a general summary of Israel's habitual rejection of God's prophets comes near the end of a recitation of the history of Israel. The history is rehearsed in order to explain the present situation of the speaker and his audience.[17]

For example, Neh 9 recounts the history of Israel as part of a formal covenant-renewal ceremony.[18] The history of God's steadfastness is told from creation to Abraham to the exodus to the giving of the law (vv. 6–15). It is in the wilderness where the people begin to disobey God's commandments. But Yahweh remains faithful to the covenant, sustaining them in the wilderness and giving them the promised land (vv. 16–25). In the land, the people again disobey God by casting the law behind their backs and killing the prophets (v. 26). Because of this, Yahweh "gave them into the hands of their enemies, who made them suffer" (v. 27). Although this cycle repeats during Israel's tenure in the land—disobedience, punishment, salvation, disobedience, and so on—God patiently warns them through the prophets, "yet they would not listen" (v. 30c). This narrated history explains the present post-exilic situation. Ezra says: "Here we are slaves to this day—slaves in the land that you gave to our ancestors to enjoy its fruit and its good gifts. Its rich yield goes to the kings whom you have set over us because of our sins; they have power also over our bodies and over our livestock at their pleasure, and we are in great distress" (vv. 36–37). As soon as the account arrives at the present, the covenant is ratified anew: "Because of all of this we make a firm agreement in writing" (v. 38) to "walk in God's law, which was given by Moses the servant of God, and to observe and do all the commandments of the statutes" (Neh 10:29). Ezra recounts the tumultuous covenantal history that brought Israel to its current status not as masters of their promised land but as vassal slaves to the Persian Empire. In a sense, Nehemiah asks, "How did it come to this?" His explanation draws on notions of communal blame: We did it to ourselves. God is steadfast, but we disobey. God punishes with the sword of other nations because we have accrued disobedience through several generations.

Similarly, at the end of the rehearsal of Israel's history in 2 Chronicles, the historian summarizes the past to explain the present: "The Lord, God of their ancestors, sent persistently to them by his messengers, because he had compassion on his people and on his dwelling place; but they kept mocking the messengers of God, despising his words, and scoffing at prophets, until the wrath of God against his people became so great that there was no remedy. Therefore, he brought up against them the king of the Chaldeans" (2 Chr 36:15–17a). In both cases, the authors understand the national calamity of exile in terms of covenantal theology. The result is self-blame: we suffered crisis not because God was unfaithful to the covenant but because *we* were unfaithful.[19] In the logic of these texts, Israel is characterized as unfaithful when it throws off the words of the Law and spurns the message of the prophets. As a result, Israel is called to commit itself to renewing the covenant and promising to be faithful.

Second Temple Jewish texts such as *Jub.* 1.12, *T. Levi* 16.2, and the *Damascus Document* 1.15 also understand the exile in light of Israel's continued disobedience—summarized by their rejection of the messengers of God. Even the Jewish historian, Josephus—a poster child for Homi Bhabha's notions of hybridity and colonial mimicry—engages in covenantal theologizing when he suggests throughout the *Jewish War* that God appointed the Romans to punish Israel for the excesses of the zealots.

The Murder of Zechariah

In his book, *The Intertextual Jesus,* Dale Allison has shown the depth and breadth of Q's close engagement with the Hebrew Scriptures.[20] Allison suggests that the two *Sophia* oracles in Q 11:49–51 and 13:34–35 mirror the text of 2 Chr 24 (vv. 17–22, 25).[21] As Allison outlines, the Chronicler presents the murder and avenging of Zechariah the son of Jehoiada in the following sequence: (1) sending prophets; (2) stoning them; (3) spilling innocent blood; (4) in the house of God; (5) the blood requires avenging;

(6) communal judgment; (7) Jerusalem forsaken. Q 11:49–51 and 13:34–35 have a similar structure, which suggests that 2 Chr 24 serves as a typological precedent for Q's theologizing about communal blame and communal punishment in light of the destruction of Jerusalem.[22]

A similar process of theologizing appears in the Jewish exegetical and haggadic traditions about the first destruction of Jerusalem. In several texts, Zechariah's blood seethes on the ground of the temple because it was not covered with dust as directed by Lev 17:13.[23] The blood is put to rest after the captain of Nebuchadnezzar's guard, Neburzaradan (2 Kgs 25:8), enters the temple and murders more than eighty thousand Israelites there. He attempts to appease the blood because, under threat of torture, the people admit that they killed Zechariah. They say, "He was a prophet who reproved us, so we rose against him and killed him, and for several years now his blood has not stopped seething."[24] Josephus also links the death of Zechariah to the destruction of Jerusalem by the Babylonians; Zechariah was killed because he prophesied the coming disaster.[25] In an interesting parallel to Q's use of Zechariah and Ps 117:26, *Midrash Num.* 30.15 suggests that the murder of Zechariah caused the Shekinah to leave the temple. *Genesis Rabbah* links the blood of Abel to the blood of Zechariah in three ways: both cry out for revenge, both are in the plural in the Hebrew, and thus both refer to the blood of all their descendents as well.[26] This resembles Q's view that the guilt for innocent blood accrues across generations. Because of the many points of contact between midrashic traditions of 2 Chr 24 and Q, it is clear that Q 11:49–51 is a good example of "Jewish traditions regarding the Temple, and the reasons why it was destroyed."[27]

The Biographies of the Prophets

All of the texts I have mentioned, as well as several early Christian ones,[28] characterize Israel's disobedience to God as a history of killing the prophets of God. However, stories about Israel's murdering of prophets are largely absent from the Hebrew Scriptures. There are a few—such as the prophets killed by Jezebel in 1 Kings and Uriah killed by Jehoiakim mentioned in the book of Jeremiah. It is later texts, however, that tell of the murder of Israel's great prophets. For example, the *Lives of the Prophets* recounts the innocent deaths (at the hands of other Israelites) of Isaiah, Jeremiah, Ezekiel, Micah, Amos, and, of course, Zechariah son of Jehoiada—who is not specifically called a prophet in 2 Chr 24.

This suggests that the trajectory of the motif of the rejection of the prophets begins with the general summarizing of covenantal history apparent in Neh 9 and 2 Chr 36 and proceeds later to biographical details of the deaths of the great prophets, killed by the hand or plan of Israelite kings or priests.

This trajectory coincides with the increased centrality of the traditions of Israel's prophets in the Second Temple period. William Schniedewind has identified a crucial development in evaluating fidelity to God's law that helps to explain this coincidence.[29] Chronicles and Ezra-Nehemiah, according to Schniedewind, both highlight the written Law in their evaluation of history and in this sense are Deuteronomistic. These texts, however, also introduce a non-Deuteronomic innovation: "employing the prophets as critical voices for evaluating fidelity to God."[30] As a result, the prophets become equally central for conveying the word of Yahweh, a process clearly set out in *m. Avot*'s chain of tradition: "Moses received Torah from Sinai and delivered it to Joshua, and Joshua to the Elders, and the Elders to the Prophets, and the Prophets delivered it to the men of the Great Synagogue." Schniedewind rightly points out that "both the priests and the laity, both the written Torah and the Oral Torah, and both the Sadducees and the Pharisees, appropriated the prophets as a voice supporting their view of history."[31]

Can we imagine a trajectory of the traditions of communal blame in Q that moves from (1) reflection on the communal experience of Jewish suffering at the hands of the Romans; (2) to traditional reflections on communal suffering and blame; (3) to the notion that Jews are directly responsible for the death of the prophet Jesus who called Israel to covenantal obedience? If this is correct, then the progressive move in the gospel traditions toward Jewish responsibility for the death of Jesus reflects a growing effort to make Jesus' biography fit the bill of a prophet who is martyred by his own people, a crime that culminates in God handing over the nation to Roman domination. Within this trajectory, collective "Jewish" responsibility for the death of Jesus and for the persecution of those who carry on his message grows up out of a Jewish covenantal tradition of self-blame for communal crisis rather than from some experience of actual "Jewish" violence.

Conclusion

Once we have made some effort to see "the other estate"—in this case, Rome and not Antigua—at the edges of Q's rhetoric of communal blame and suffering, the revolutionary writings of the early "postcolonialist" thinkers begin to resonate with early Jesus traditions like Q. For example, Albert Memmi, Franz Fanon, and Aimé Césaire passionately describe the many violences of colonization on both the colonized and the colonizer. Memmi speaks of the tendency among the colonized to take the blame for their own suffering.[32] Fanon speaks of the intense efforts of the colonized to persuade themselves that history still continues and that they are somehow responsible for their own history.[33] Césaire points out how local religious traditions attempt to integrate the power of the colonizer into the divine plan with the result that the abuses of power by the colonizer are no longer seen as brutality so much as divine will.[34] These observations ring true for the texts that we have been investigating.

Perhaps it was the experience of communal suffering at the hands of Roman imperial occupation that burned at the heart of Q's theologizing about communal blame. Perhaps the community of Q was moved *not only* by the brutal crucifixion of one righteous and prophetic Jew, but also by the deaths of *thousands* of Jews at the hands of the Romans in the first century C.E. Perhaps it was the smoking ruins of rebellious Jerusalem that brought the Q people to ask: "How did it come to this?" And perhaps it was their memory of Jesus teaching about the *basileia* of God and his brutal crucifixion on a Roman cross that brought them to answer that question in their own particular way.

Postscript

Working with undergraduates can be an enlightening experience. Since I presented a version of this essay in the Consultation on Violence Among Jews and Christians, I have had two telling encounters with students over the issue of Christian anti-Judaism. In a course on Christian history, we were reading Justin's *Dialogue with Trypho* and discussing how Justin attempts to create boundaries between the categories "Jew" and "Christian." The students, offended by Justin's blanket statements about Jews, pointed to Justin's accusation that all Jews were responsible for the death of Jesus and the persecution of the Christians (16) as an especially egregious passage. For the following class I asked them to review the *Dialogue* and to explain why Christian anti-Judaism arose. Despite their earlier probing comments and the ensuing discussion, the students answered in a straightforward and uniform fashion: Christian anti-Judaism arose because the Jews killed Jesus and because they persecuted Christians. My students had transformed the *example* of anti-Judaism into the *explanation* for anti-Judaism. The logic was disturbingly circular: the Christians started saying the Jews killed Jesus because the Jews killed Jesus. The Christians started saying anti-Jewish things because the Jews were anti-Christian.

This anecdote underlines the historicizing power of the gospel narratives. The gospel traditions progressively construct a fiction of communal action—that "the Jews" killed Jesus. This totalized group action results in blame assessed across the generations in Matthew's chilling redaction of Mark's trial scene, where Pilate washes his hands clean as the crowd exclaims that Jesus' blood will be on their hands and on the hands of their children (Matt 27:24–25). As we know, this scene is now replayed for the millions of viewers who attend Mel Gibson's movie, *The Passion of the Christ*.[35] After this movie came out, one of my students shared that he enjoyed it and declared that it "wasn't anti-Semitic." He continued: "It does show that the Jews kill Jesus, but, well, that's what happened." I would not be surprised by this claim except for the fact that this student had taken two courses with me, one in Bible and one in early Christian history. In both classes, we had devoted many hours to the issue of Christian anti-Judaism—apparently to little lasting effect in this case.

Biblical scholars and theologians must continue to engage in both historical research and ethical reflection on this form of community profiling. John Dominic Crossan points to the ethical imperative of applying power analysis to the ongoing interpretation of the passion story:

As long as Christians were the marginalized and disenfranchised ones, such passion fiction about Jewish responsibility and Roman innocence did nobody much harm. But, once the Roman Empire became Christian, that fiction turned lethal. In the light of later Christian anti-Judaism and eventually of genocidal anti-Semitism, it is no longer possible in retrospect to think of that passion fiction as relatively benign propaganda. However explicable its origins, defensible its invectives, and understandable its motives among Christians fighting for survival, its repetition has now become the longest lie, and, for our own integrity, we Christians must at last name it as such.[36]

Projects such as the Consultation on Violence Among Jews and Christians and the effort to open up new avenues of inquiry following the insights of postcolonial,[37] feminist,[38] and Jewish scholars[39] can only help in this vital ongoing work.

Notes

1. Edward Said, *Culture and Imperialism* (New York: Knopf, 1993), 84–97.

2. Ibid., 89–90.

3. For the text of Q, the postulated source common to Matthew and Luke, I use the reconstructed text from the International Q Project. See James M. Robinson, Paul Hoffman, and John S. Kloppenborg, eds., *The Critical Edition of Q* (Hermeneia; Leuven: Peeters; Minneapolis: Fortress Press, 2000). According to common practice, I cite Q by Lukan numbering.

4. For a summary of the violent situation of first-century Palestine, see Richard A. Horsley, *Bandits, Prophets, and Messiahs* (2d ed.; Harrisburg, Pa.: Trinity Press International, 1999), 29–47.

5. I have not translated the Greek word σοφία (wisdom) so that its gender remains apparent. The feminine σοφία more clearly brings to mind the personification of God in the Hebrew Scriptures and Apocrypha (Prov 8:1–36 and 9:1–6 and Wis 7:22–8:1) than the neutral and abstract notion of God's wisdom. I have capitalized *Sophia* because God's Wisdom is personified in Q as a parent who has children (Q 7:35) and as one who sends out prophets and sages (Q 11:49).

6. See Robinson et al., *Critical Edition,* 284–88. I have made some changes in the translation.

7. See, for example, Alan Kirk, "The Memory of Violence and the Death of Jesus in Q" (paper presented at the annual meeting of the American Academy of Religion/ Society of Biblical Literature, November 2003).

8. See, for example, Arland Jacobson, *The First Gospel: An Introduction to Q* (Sonoma, Calif.: Polebridge, 1992).

9. While I agree with Michael Cook's criticisms of the apologetic tendencies of the "in-house squabbling" explanation of New Testament anti-Jewish polemic, he overlooks the fact that many historians who reconstruct such internecine conflict in the gospels also agree with him that anti-Judaism in the New Testament is "not a *Jewish* problem but a *Christian* problem" (305). Cook's own historical reconstruction posits a split between Jews and "Christians" at an unlikely early date. See Michael Cook, "The New Testament: Confronting Its Impact on Jewish-Christian Relations," in *Biblical Studies Alternatively* (ed. Suzanne Scholz; New Jersey: Prentice Hall, 2003), 291–307, esp. 298–99.

10. See Robinson et al., *Critical Edition,* 282–83.

11. I agree with Josef Verheyden's argument that there is no indication that the current audience ("this generation") murders prophets. See Josef Verheyden, "The Killing

of the Prophets in Q and the Deuteronomistic Tradition: Some Reflexions" (presented at the annual meeting of the American Academy of Religion/Society of Biblical Literature, November 2002).

12. Luke's ἐκζητηθῇ points directly to blood required for blood spilled (see, for example, LXX Gen 9:5, 42:22; 2 Sam 4:11, and Pol. *Phil* 2.1). Matthew's ἔλθῃ ἐφ᾽ ὑμᾶς includes punishment for the wider range of suffering listed in Matt 23:34 (including crucifixion, scourging, and persecution). The IQP prefers Luke's ἐκζητηθῇ (see Robinson et al., *Critical Edition*, 286).

13. Robinson et al., *Critical Edition*, 420–22. For a presentation of the arguments in favor of placing Q 13:34–34 after Q 11:49–51, see James M. Robinson, "The Sequence of Q: The Lament over Jerusalem," in *Von Jesus zum Christus* (ed. Rudulf Hoppe and Ulrich Busse; Berlin: de Gruyter, 1998), 225–60.

14. For dating the completed Q to the time of the Jewish War, see Matti Myllykoski, "The Social History of Q and the Jewish War," in *Symbols and Strata: Essays on the Sayings Gospel Q* (Göttingen: Vandenhoeck & Ruprecht, 1996), 143–99.

15. Odil Hannes Steck, *Israel und das gewaltsame Geschick der Propheten* (WMANT 23; Neukirchen-Vluyn: Neukirchener Verlag, 1967).

16. There are a few other cases of violence against prophets, but these are not interpreted as evidence of Israel's common disobedience: prophets killed by Jezebel (1 Kgs 18:4, 13; 19:10, 14); the murder of Zechariah son of Jehoiada (2 Chr 24:17–25); and the murder of Uriah by Jehoiakim (Jer 26:20–23). Interestingly, the second case proves useful to Q and other early Jewish reflection on Israel's first-century suffering.

17. In Jer 2, the prophet frames Judah's infidelity to its covenant with Yahweh in the terms of a broken marriage contract. In 2 Chr 36, the Chronicler summarizes all the history that has been recounted in the book as an explanation of the coming of the Babylonians.

18. See Klaus Balzer, "The Tora of Moses and the Book of Isaiah as Prophetic History" (presented at the annual meeting of the American Academy of Religion/Society of Biblical Literature, November 2002).

19. Jeremiah has a similar reflection on covenant in the form of a marriage contract between Israel (the northern kingdom) and Yahweh and between Judah and Yahweh. Israel has broken her marriage vows and has been divorced (witness the destruction of the north by Assyria in 721 B.C.E.). Jeremiah suggests that the marriage covenant between Judah and Yahweh has also been broken because Judah cavorts with Assyria and Egypt. The oracles imply that only destruction can come from such infidelity.

20. Dale Allison, *The Intertextual Jesus* (Harrisburg, Pa.: Trinity Press International, 2000), 84–87 and 149–52.

21. Ibid., 150.

22. Ibid.

23. For example, *b. Git.* 57b; *Lam. Rab.* proem 23; *Eccl. Rab.* 3.19.

24. *Lam. Rab.* proem 23.

25. Josephus, *Ant.* 9.169.

26. *Gen. Rab.* 22.9.

27. Arland Jacobson, "Q and the Deuteronomistic Tradition" (presented at the annual meeting of the American Academy of Religion/Society of Biblical Literature, November 2002). Jacobson helpfully discusses several of these texts in his analysis.

28. See 1 Thess 2:14–16; Acts 7:52; *Barn.* 5.2; and Justin, *Trypho* 16.

29. William M. Schniedewind, "The Legacy of Deuteronomy in the 2nd Temple Period" (presented at the annual meeting of the American Academy of Religion/Society of Biblical Literature, November 2002).

30. Ibid. This innovation coincides with the "textualization of the prophets themselves in Second Temple literature."

31. Ibid.

32. Albert Memmi, *The Colonizer and the Colonized* (New York: Orion Press, 1965; repr., Boston: Beacon, 1991), 87.

33. Franz Fanon, *The Wretched of the Earth* (New York: Grove Press, 1963), 54.

34. Aimé Césaire, *Discourse on Colonialism* (trans. Joan Pinkham; New York: Monthly Review Press, 1972), 39–42.

35. Gibson leaves untranslated the call for Jesus' blood to be on the generations of Jews. However, he does include the words that Jesus speaks to Pilate in John 19:11: "the one who handed me over to you is guilty of a greater sin."

36. John Dominic Crossan, *Who Killed Jesus? Exposing the Roots of Anti-Semitism in the Gospel Story of the Death of Jesus* (San Francisco: HarperSanFrancisco, 1995), xi–xii.

37. See, for example, R. S. Sugirtharajah, *Postcolonial Criticism and Biblical Interpretation* (Oxford: Oxford University Press, 2002).

38. See, for example, Elisabeth Schüssler Fiorenza, *Jesus and the Politics of Interpretation* (New York: Continuum, 2000).

39. See, for example, the contributions to Paula Fredriksen and Adele Reinhartz, eds., *Jesus, Judaism, and Christian Anti-Judaism* (Louisville, Ky.: Westminster/John Knox, 2002).

3

Collateral Damage:
Jesus and Jezebel in the Jewish War

John W. Marshall

"Violence *among* Jews and Christians"—taken from the title of the SBL session where this volume originated—makes possible a necessary condition of my investigation: to treat the inner religious violence of John's Apocalypse without presupposing Christianity as a distinct and taxonomically equal entity to which Judaism can be compared, contrasted, and set into relations of influence, negotiation, and conflict. Lacking "Christians," the Apocalypse cannot depict violence between Christians and Jews, but this should not remove the question of inner religious violence. Put baldly, I don't see any violence between Jews and Christians in John's Apocalypse, because I don't see any Christians.[1] Violence within the in-group, however, is not lacking in the scene depicted in Revelation. A shocking text from John's Apocalypse depicts a chilling threat of violence that is my entry into the circumstances and inner religious conflicts that decisively condition Revelation's treatment of differences *within* the movement of Jews in Asia Minor that John understands as his community.

The following words are attributed to "the Son of God," Jesus, in Rev 2:22 and the beginning of verse 23: "Watch, I'll shove her on a bed, and make her lovers suffer terribly, unless they turn away from what she does. And I'm going to kill her children, dead." Though this translation is accurate in its particulars and powerful in its vividness, it may not be as familiar as the Revised Standard Version's rendering: "Behold, I will throw her on a sickbed, and those who commit adultery with her I will throw into great tribulation, unless they repent of her doings; and I will strike her children dead." In removing the liturgical Sunday best that this text usually wears, I have attempted to make clear its violent intervention

35

in a religious rivalry within a subaltern group. Jesus, referred to in this particular message as the Son of God (Rev 2:18), is talking about a woman that the book of Revelation calls "Jezebel." It is in this text, in this threat, that I see the situation of the Apocalypse exemplified, the conditions of its composition distilled, and the tableau of its origins brought into sharp focus.

Before moving on then to explaining how this threat encapsulates the compositional context of John's Apocalypse, it is necessary to lay out several of the positions and evaluations that undergird my reading and the choice of this site to examine the question of insider violence in the Apocalypse. Three questions may set the agenda here: In what historical context did John compose? In what religious context did John formulate his vision? And in what political formation did the exigence for John's writing arise? Thus I will first sketch a case for the wartime context of Revelation; second, attempt to map the situation of Revelation in social and religious terms; and third, endeavor to bring to bear on Revelation a mode and theory of historiography that can illuminate a key cross-cultural phenomenon that conditions the entire setting, exigence, and stance of the book. I have in mind historiography informed by postcolonial analyses and theorizing in order to treat the colonial situation in which Revelation was conceived, composed, and received more satisfactorily.

Wartime Context

Axes of Violence

Violence in John's Apocalypse runs along several axes: Babylon and the Angels, Michael and the Dragon, the two witnesses and the people of the Great City, the Son of God and the children of Jezebel, the word of God and the Gentiles. These are all terms from within John's Apocalypse: transforming these terms and patterns to entities and relationships in John's social world is a complex endeavor. Overwhelmingly these depictions of violence elaborate a conflict between, on the one hand, the Holy City and its divine patron, and, on the other hand, the Great City, which is Babylon and Rome and of which Satan is the patron. Almost always, the violence in the Apocalypse is a reconfiguration of this conflict worked out though a variety of literary proxies. Violence in Revelation is either the direct product of this clash of divine powers, or it is the well-modulated and considered suffering permitted to the people in their

destined fulfillment of the eschatological program. The sole exception is
the conflict over false teachers in the messages to the seven assemblies in
which figures under the name of Jezebel and Balaam as well as a group
called the Nicolaitans receive sharp condemnations. The threats of violence reach their apex with Jezebel. But even though the threat against
Jezebel stands as a nearly singular depiction of inner religious violence, I
argue that the circumstances that generate the depiction of violence
against the outsider (figured as Babylon) also generate the depiction of the
violence against the insider (equally figured as Jezebel).

Date

Dating the Apocalypse is a task fraught with uncertainty, and the more
precise one's hypothesis, the smaller the circle of agreement it can command. In spite of this eminently sensible observation, I find myself per-
suaded by quite a narrow window and quite a specific circumstance: the
Jewish Diaspora in western Asia Minor during the latter stages of the Jewish War, in the long year, 69 C.E., or immediately following. I have made a
more extensive argument elsewhere;[2] here a brief sketch of the case must
suffice. First, it is widely agreed that the reign of Nero and its chaotic
aftermath make the most plausible and simple referents when interpreting
the numbering of emperors in chapter 17 and the gematria in chapter 13.
There is no need for starting in the middle of the sequence or finding reasons to omit emperors. Second, the scene at the beginning of chapter 11
where the outer zones of the Holy City are given over to the Gentiles is
eminently understandable in the midst of the Jewish War. Third, I find the
arguments about the value of Irenaeus's poorly informed testimony in the
latter half of the second century unpersuasive and the use of the term
Babylon insufficient to distinguish the aftermath of the war from its
course. These are merely topics and do not constitute an argument, but
they should illuminate the larger understanding that undergirds a date in
late 69 or early 70 C.E.

Cultural/Political Context

Such a date, however, is quite significant for Jewish communities in the
ancient world. The armies of Rome had surrounded the Holy City and
seemed to teeter between overrunning the temple of God and turning in
on themselves in a storm of self-destruction, marching away from the

Holy City to continue the conflagration that engulfed northern Italy itself as emperor slew emperor in dizzying succession.[3] In the uncertainty of the long year, which Tacitus in a fit of Roman eschatological pessimism describes as looking by all accounts like the empire's last,[4] John's community sought to make sense of the violence of Rome upon Jerusalem and to reconcile it with their hope in the power of their God and his Christ. Understanding this specific situation in more general terms and exploring the relation between the shape of this situation and the instance of insider violence in the Apocalypse of John is the task of this essay.

Religious Map

Polythetic Taxonomy

Moving from a chronological, geographical, and political mapping to a religious mapping, I need to emphasize that the glib phrase "I don't see any Christians" conceals an utterly serious claim: namely, that applying the term "Christian" to the author or initial audience of the Apocalypse has no justification in a nonconfessional historical endeavor. The methodological foundation of this serious claim is crucial and the stakes are substantial.

I do not claim that there is no figure called "Christ" in the Apocalypse, only that the move to a new religious formation suitable for naming and framing and comparison *with* Judaism rather than understanding *within* Judaism has not taken place. Nor does such a divide occupy John's attention or motivate his writing. I am convinced that the ubiquitous move to name the Apocalypse as a Christian document and to interpret it as such is a gross category error, that it proceeds from a methodologically untenable understanding of the constitution of a religion and the enterprise of taxonomy in the study of religion, and that the category itself serves primarily to introduce a distortion into the interpretation of the Apocalypse that is at odds with disciplined historical-critical inquiry. On the basis of Jonathan Z. Smith's work on taxonomies of religion, and on the basis of the constituent elements of religion that Smith's work implies,[5] I have made the argument that the usual understanding of the book of Revelation as a Christian rather than a Jewish document is an initial error that undermines the entire enterprise of historical-critical interpretation. Again, skeletal summary must stand in for substantial argumentation.[6]

"Conflict with Jews"

The result of these convictions, and the historical-critical arguments that support them, is that the very idea of "conflict with Jews" is a red herring in the interpretation of the Apocalypse.[7] The synagogue of Satan passages are arguments, not descriptions, over what constitutes authentic Judaism, made with reference to food offered to idols, not with reference to the status of Jesus. It is in no way fair to say, with the majority of commentators, that when John says his opponents *are not* Jews that he means they *are* Jews and that his conviction is that Christians are the true Jews. This is the Gentile Christianity of Justin Martyr retrojected onto an Asian Jew devoted to Jesus. Similarly the conflict in chapter 11, in which the two witnesses are slain in the streets of the Great City, is, as several commentators recognize, an indictment of Rome rather than a criticism of Jerusalem. There are no other pillars in an argument that "conflict with the Jews" animates Revelation, and these pillars turn out to be hollow.[8] In contrast, the conclusion of Revelation clears up the matter. There's all the violence anyone in his or her right mind could stomach, but when the losers in this eschatological fantasy are being thrown in the fire or carved by the bridegroom at his own wedding and served up to the birds of heaven, Jews are nowhere to be found. The list of opponents is extensive, but Jews are not on it.

This context for viewing the Apocalypse of John constitutes a substantial departure from common scholarly strategies of reading. The most methodologically significant is holding the category "Christian" in abeyance—not only refraining from naming the group under examination as "Christian," but also forgoing the common strategy of formulating Christian problems that John's text is assumed to address. In strictly chronological terms, I have advocated an early date in concert with many scholars who date all or part of the Apocalypse to the period of the Jewish War. Combining these insights makes it possible for the significance of the Jewish War for the Jewish Diaspora and Rome's efforts to suppress one of the ethnic revolts that were endemic to its empire to rise to prominence.[9] It is under these conditions and circumstances, methodological, temporal, and political, that I read the threats against Jezebel, her associates, and her children.

Jesus and Jezebel 1: The Characters

The question of inner religious violence in the book of Revelation comes into focus in 2:22–23, where Jezebel is accused of sexual immorality and of eating food that has been offered to idols. Let me recall to you the text I began with—John's visionary report of the message of the Son of God concerning a prophetess that he calls Jezebel—in a more extensive quotation:

> I have this against you: that you tolerate the woman Jezebel who calls herself a prophet and teaches and misleads my servants to practice sexual immorality and to eat food that has been offered to idols. I gave her time to give it up, but she doesn't want to turn away from her sexual immorality. Watch, I'll shove her on a bed, and make her lovers suffer terribly, unless they turn away from what she does. And I'm going to kill her children, dead.

Here the conditions of the Apocalypse are brought into sharp focus.

The two characters of this text, Jesus and Jezebel, are absolutely asymmetrical within the Apocalypse. The speaker in this text is ostensibly Jesus, identified in the preface to the message as "the Son of God," giving one of his messages to the angels of seven assemblies of Asia Minor. Clearly the "Son of God" here is the revealer figure of chapter 1, characterized by John as "the ruler of the kings of the earth," and who ranges across the action of John's apocalyptic vision rather than entering at a single point. He leads his followers, pure and holy, in imagined combat against the forces of Babylon and Rome, portrayed as illegitimate, unholy, and impure. Jezebel appears only once as a member of a triad of internal enemies that populate the messages to the angels of the seven assemblies— Jezebel, Balaam, and the Nicolaitans. Jezebel, of course, is John's slanderous name for a figure whom we cannot specify in her own terms. By naming her "Jezebel," John ties her to the Jezebel of the Hebrew Bible, the foreign-born wife of King Ahab. She leads her husband to worship Baal and idols (1 Kgs 16:31; 18:18; 21:25–26), opposes the prophets of the Lord and is responsible for their deaths (1 Kgs 18:4, 13; 19:2ff.), supports the prophets of Baal and Asherah (1 Kgs 18:19), and practices sorcery and sexual immorality (2 Kgs 9:22). This characterization of Jezebel is drawn mainly from 1 Kings in the Hebrew Bible, but the prophetic messenger of Elisha in 2 Kings who anoints Jehu the king after Ahab also makes the following prophecy:

> And you shall strike down the house of Ahab your master, that I
> may avenge on Jezebel the blood of my servants the prophets, and
> the blood of all the servants of the LORD. For the whole house of
> Ahab shall perish; and I will cut off from Ahab every male, bond or
> free, in Israel. And I will make the house of Ahab like the house of
> Jeroboam the son of Nebat, and like the house of Baasha the son of
> Ahijah. And the dogs shall eat Jezebel in the territory of Jezreel, and
> none shall bury her. (2 Kgs 9:7–10)

The bitter prophecy of Elisha's messenger, that the blood of the prophets
rests on Jezebel, and that she shall die unburied and eaten by dogs, match-
es the vividness of John's own visionary indictment. It is between Jezebel
and Jesus—Jezebel whom John has named so slanderously and Jesus
whom he has figured as Son of God, Son of Man, the holder of the key of
David—that the conflict of John with others inside his community
reaches its apex in the threat on which I have chosen to focus.

This threat of violence *within* the group, that is to say within John's
setting in Judaism in Asia Minor, stands as a nearly singular contrast to
the dominant pattern within Revelation of threatened, implied, or depicted
violence against the outsiders: namely, the Gentiles who have free commerce with Rome. John writes in the course of what looked like Rome's
fateful disintegration, with the hope that the revolutionary Jews of
Jerusalem would, with divine intervention, be vindicated. With the benefit
of hindsight, few could share John's analysis.

Collateral Damage

Given these conditions that drive me to focus on the threats against
Jezebel as the clearest depiction of insider violence in the book of Revelation, what can explain the bitterness of the condemnation and the intensi-
ty of the threat? Traditional answers to questions of this type dwell on the
way in which apocalyptic channels for the construction of knowledge and
eschatological scenarios for the rectification of imperfection raise the
stakes in argument, drawing to shrill pitch the conflicts that so regularly
afflict new religious movements. Others have focused on the well-known
fervor of insider conflict. Jonathan Z. Smith's description of the offense of
the proximate other captures some of the heat generated in the crucible of
insider conflict—"While the 'other' may be perceived as being either
LIKE-US or NOT-LIKE-US, he is, in fact, most problematic when he is

TOO-MUCH-LIKE-US, or when he claims to BE-US."[10] David Frankfurter has explored John's strident efforts to differentiate himself from his
"other," specifically with regard to the synagogue of Satan passages,
observing that proximate position and fuzzy borders generate rhetoric of
extreme distance and sharp borders.[11] Frankfurter has substantially
advanced our understanding of the conflict. We can, however, connect
these insights to the specific chronological, geographical, and cultural
reconstruction of John's situation that I have advocated: specifically the
"long year," 69 C.E., during the larger Jewish War of 66–70 C.E.; the Jewish Diaspora; and hybrid community in colonial empire. It is this latter
characterization of the cultural context that invites the application of
postcolonial theory.

Postcolonialism

In the last fifteen years, a body of scholarship has grown up that theorizes
the phenomenon of colonization as a basic form of human interaction
that conditions particular circumstances as powerfully and pervasively as
the objects of other analyses do: as pervasively as race, as powerfully as
gender, as persistently as class. By and large such scholarship has been oriented to the last five centuries of European colonial endeavor, and a large
part of it has been devoted to the reconsideration and reinterpretation of
literary works—from both the colony and metropole—with a disciplined
attention to the historical and discursive dynamics of colonization.
Other trajectories work in a more social-historical mode, most prominently the subaltern studies group focused especially on peasant politics of South Asia. The heroes of this movement—revered, tilted at,
dismissed, and cited as academic heroes—include Homi Bhabha, Gayatri
Spivak, Ranjit Guha, Edward Said, Partha Chaterjee, along with a cast of
figures known often under the rubric of postmodernists. Two analytical
concepts elaborated by postcolonialists can illuminate the insider violence
of the Apocalypse of John: the first is hybridity; the second concerns the
role of women as tokens of argumentation in colonial settings.

Hybridity

The notion of hybridity encompasses several locations in the literal and
social geography of the colonial encounter. It is the condition of creative and
contentious mixing of traditions and cultures that the colonized subject

must negotiate.[12] It flowers in the colonial elite's value-laden embrace of elements of the subject culture, seen also in a slightly less hierarchical mode in the foreignness of the expatriate community. "Hybridity" also names the compromised condition of colonial authority. Diaspora is a paradigmatic location of hybridity as the dispersed negotiate what it means to be themselves in a new space. New spaces cannot support old selves and the tensions of maintenance and modification, fraught always with questions of value and hypotheses of essence, afflict the colonized in the homeland and, just as surely, those scattered in dispersion.

Within postcolonial analyses, the concept of hybridity is deployed in the analysis of a variety of situations. In Homi Bhabha's influential development of the concept in "Signs Taken for Wonders," his focus is on the contradictory movements within strategies of maintaining colonial domination.[13] Hybridity names primarily the comprised condition of the colonizers' authority, but also the changed circumstances of the colonized's subjectivity. The case that I have in mind here—the threats against Jezebel and her children—takes a different shape, but can be illuminated by the second element of Bhabha's analytic apparatus when we include also a primary source that has animated Bhabha's thinking on hybridity: Frantz Fanon's reflection on the colonial state of Algeria.[14]

Fanon's analysis of the colonial situation focused on the agency and the possibilities that the colonized can deploy, with substantial attention to justifying the particular, and sometimes unpalatable, forms that colonial resistance may take. Fanon knows, and Bhabha learns from him and others, that the colonial or subaltern situation is not so simple and that the operation of desire in colonial contexts is thoroughly interwoven with the relations of power that characterize the colonial situation. Fanon describes the colonial subject as double-minded, simultaneously scorning and wanting to displace and replace the colonizer, an "envious man," in Fanon's own words.[15] Fanon describes the colonial context as forcing a "dichotomy . . . upon the whole people."[16] Most specifically relevant to the situation of John and Jezebel, Fanon acknowledges the *relation* of violence within the in-group as it struggles with the pressure of colonial domination.[17]

The conflict that animates the critique of Jezebel is well known to be "eating food offered to idols" (Rev 2:20). This question of what is licit to eat and what are the ramifications of transgressing the boundary of permissible food is raised to high stakes by the condition of the Jewish War and the situation of the Jewish Diaspora during that war. When the armies of the empire are laying siege to the Holy City Jerusalem, how can a Jew conduct daily life in the Gentile cities without contamination or betrayal? Obviously, there are more answers to this question than John is willing to countenance. This condition itself is comparable to other examples of the pressures diasporas face during wartime and in this case is a subset of the larger condition of colonial domination. John, and his literary proxy the Son of God, focus such strident threats against Jezebel and her children because of the conflicted positions that characterize subaltern groups in colonial situations.[18]

The underlying concern that gives currency to the question of eating food offered to idols is the topic of purity. Here is the intersection with the concept of hybridity—perhaps "collision" is the more accurate term—and it becomes clear how John's commitment to purity[19] is a catalyst for conflict in the face of the hybridity that colonization engenders. Between John and Jezebel, this issue of food offered to idols stands as a divider, a litmus test of the authenticity of Judaism. For Jezebel, we must infer that, inasmuch as the accusation of eating food offered to idols is accurate, she did not understand that action as constituting a departure from her understanding of an authentic Judaism. Here are Celsus's squabbling frogs, arguing over food at a fevered pitch when they stand together participating in a massive innovation within Judaism that treats Jesus as the viceroy of God. This conflict has been cast as a Paulinist configuration of devotion to Jesus and John's form, one less oriented to opening a wide path to Gentiles. Perhaps this is the genealogy of the conflict between John and Jezebel. Its mechanics, its source of power, however, is the pressure of subalternity. Frantz Fanon's description of the self-destructive release of the native's "muscular tension"[20] finds an ancient example in the conflict of John and Jezebel.

Arguing with Women

The second analytical avenue—formulated earlier as "the role of women as tokens of argumentation in colonial settings"—proceeds from the gendered quality of the other accusation against Jezebel, namely the accusation that she undertakes illegitimate sexual unions (πορνεῦσαι). In the colonial economy of representation, women are often positioned by men as the bearers of subaltern purity and authenticity. Obligations as the flag bearers of morality are put upon women and they are positioned by men as tokens of argumentation in anticolonial discourse. In spite of this, scholars habitually ask the following questions concerning the accusation against Jezebel of sexual impropriety: Is this metaphor? Is this a genuine feature of the opponents? Does the accusation hold a reality in addition to its metaphorical power? They do not ask about the shape of the conflict in terms of gender and in combination with colonized subjectivity. The threats of the Son of God are formulated not only against Jezebel, but also against those with whom she is said to have illegitimately mixed (τοὺς μοιχεύοντας μετ' αὐτῆς). Not surprisingly, John focuses on the woman and she stands as a token of thought and argument in male discourse. In the arena of civic politics, Kate Cooper's description of the process of "thinking with virgins"[21] develops this insight for Western antiquity as she argues that men of the late antique world articulated a new discourse of sexual morality in order to circumscribe an arena of power and competition in the face of declining civic participation. Within postcolonial criticism, the deployment of women as pretexts for colonial intervention whether by contemporary theorists or colonial administrators is understood as one of the most vexing binds of the colonial and postcolonial situation. In historical terms, this phenomenon is seen preeminently in the British opposition to the practice of *sati* and strained combinations of denunciation, rationalization, and explanation that followed in response.

In Revelation, John focuses his critique of insiders on the figure of Jezebel, formulating that critique vividly as a denunciation of a woman's sexual practice. This corresponds closely to the denunciations of the outsiders—the kings of the earth—in their relations to the whore of Babylon that the book of Revelation narrates so extensively in chapter 17. John draws a female character as the conduit of contamination between the insider community and the contaminating influence of the outside, the other. She broaches the border that ought not to be crossed in John's view. In his focus on woman's sexuality and his focus on a woman as a conduit of contamination in the colonial encounter, John engages a recurrent trope of colonial relations. We see the reverse of this elsewhere in the New Testament in the exhortation of 1 Tim 5:14 that "young women should marry, bear children, and keep house so that the enemy should have no occasion to criticize." In 1 Timothy, the outsider's gaze—the Greco-Roman gaze—is the motive for rectitude among young women, whom the author positions as the community's flag bearers of virtue; in Revelation, censure of a female character's sexual activity is the most prominent criticism of practice within John's community. Whether as good wives or as paradigmatic adulteresses, female characters in both texts function as tokens of argumentation in a discourse written by and primarily for men with reference to the wider situation of colonial empire.

The insider conflict in Revelation is seen not only in the conflict with Jezebel, but also in denunciations of the figure, presumably male, of Balaam, and in condemnations of the teaching of the group named the Nicolaitans. Though the message of "the one who has the two-edged sword" to the angel of the assembly at Pergamum briefly threatens a fight against the opponents of the assembly, it comes as no surprise that the threat of violence finds its most elaborate form in the bullying of Jezebel and her followers.

Jesus and Jezebel 2: The Opposition

The opposition of male as pure to female as impure is certainly wider than the colonial context. But Revelation's version of that highly gendered opposition is overwhelmingly oriented to John's understanding of a conflict between the forces of God and Jerusalem on the one hand and the forces of Rome and the Devil on the other. The Son of God is the purveyor of purity, promising white garments and a heavenly abode to his followers, leading saints who have kept themselves "from being defiled with women" (Rev 14:4) in a war against the fornicating empire. Jezebel, figured as female and impure, represents a hybridity that John cannot tolerate because his understanding of the stakes of the conflict between Jerusalem and Rome, absolutely literally as well as figuratively, make essential difference, the difference between purity and impurity, absolutely necessary. John's Jesus has no tolerance for Jezebel and the less starkly drawn border she represents for him.

Comparisons and Conclusions

Let me step back then and try to relate these investigations to a larger set of concerns. The substance of my conclusion is that the conflict over food offered to idols, the conflict that finds its most violent expression in the threats against Jezebel, is illuminated by postcolonial analyses that attend to the specific forms of domination that can afflict subject communities, especially how subaltern communities understand their basic identities to be at stake at the most basic levels, how they are prone to turn violently on the proximate other as a means of addressing the pressures in their situation, how ideals of gender that are put to the test in front of the other's gaze can set up women as tokens of argumentation—with predictably deleterious effects.

On one hand, the death of Jesus does not function as a template for the insider violence in the Apocalypse and certainly John has no intention to cast Jezebel as an imitator of Christ, but on the other hand, the broader dynamic of the narratives of Jesus' trial with their varying degrees of exoneration offered to Pilate exemplify the divisions within subject communities under the pressures of colonial domination. Thus, in contrast to Acts or martyrological literature, for example, correspondences are much more sociological than narratological. The colonial situation creates the continuity between the sociological and the narratological and this is seen most clearly *without* an overdrawn distinction between Judaism and Christianity, implying a taxonomic equality between the two.

Jewish War

The question of the historicity of the threats against Jezebel does not lead far. There is no warrant to believe that the Son of God did come, shove Jezebel onto a bed and her lovers into great suffering, and kill her children dead. Nor is there evidence of Jezebel's repentance. What's important is that the bitterness of inner Jewish conflict in Revelation gains context in the wider phenomenon of inner Jewish conflict in the course of the Jewish War. In this most proximate realm of comparison, John's conflict with Jezebel stands as a diasporic companion to the bitter conflicts among the revolutionaries trapped within the besieged Jerusalem during the course of the Jewish War. Josephus—whose work and life, themselves, are ripe for a postcolonial analysis—describes the portents, heavenly visions, and miracles that attended the city before and during its siege as being put to use by authorities to quell dissent within the city. In his discussion of heavenly portents, revealing stars, and omens, Josephus says that "Numerous prophets, indeed, were at this period deployed by the tyrants to delude the people, by bidding them to await help from God, in order that desertions might be checked."[22] The comparison is apt, not only because of the form of the conflict and the particularities of dating the Apocalypse, but because of the role of colonial rule and visionary knowledge in both of them.[23]

Maccabean Crisis

Sensing the role of visionary knowledge in the particular shape of inner Jewish conflict under Roman hegemony invites comparison with another politically conditioned fount of apocalyptic literature in the preceding period of the Hellenistic empires, namely the Maccabean crisis.

Chapter 2 of 1 Maccabees narrates the activation of Mattathias, the father of Judas the Maccabee, as a leader of resistance to trends in Jewish life that he understood as constituting a retreat from a wholehearted embrace of Jewish practice and piety. Mattathias claims that he will make no compromise: "I and my sons and my brothers will live by the covenant of our fathers. Far be it from us to desert the law and the ordinances. We will not obey the king's words by turning aside from our religion to the right hand or to the left" (1 Macc 2:20–22). Soon after, however, a Jew reads the situation differently and offers sacrifice that Mattathias understands as a desertion of the law. Mattathias burns with anger and kills this fellow Jew on the altar itself (1 Macc 2:23–24). Subsequently, Mattathias leads a group of zealots to the wilderness and some of his allies put into practice their commitment to die rather than fight on the Sabbath (1 Macc 2:32–38). Mattathias, however, does not see things the same way and reasons that fighting on the Sabbath is not utterly impermissible. The Hasidim join him, presumably in agreement within this position, and they proceed to their next act of insider violence: killing sinners—fellow Jews—and performing forced circumcisions (1 Macc 2:42–47). The primary justification of insider violence here corresponds closely to that of the Apocalypse: relation to foreign gods. The situation is similar as well: political conflict with a ruling empire gives new currency to communal difference over relations to foreign cult.

Collateral Damage

Mattathias and John are not absolutists; each has his zones of compromise, each negotiates the difficult terrain of subservience to empire at a cost to his fellow Jews, but each seems absolutely sure of the error of those insiders who do not agree. And the violence with which each defends those seemingly absolute convictions is chilling. I suggest that the insider violence inside John's Apocalypse constitutes "collateral damage" in the larger confrontation that is endemic to colonial empire.

Notes

1. I develop this argument in John W. Marshall, *Parables of War: Reading John's Jewish Apocalypse* (Studies in Christianity and Judaism/Études sur le christianisme et le judaïsm; Waterloo, Ont.: Wilfrid Laurier University Press, 2001).

2. Ibid., 88–97.

3. See accounts in Tacitus and Suetonius as well as the standard treatment by Kenneth Wellesley, *The Long Year A.D. 69* (London: Paul Elek, 1975).

4. Tacitus, *Hist.* 1.11.

5. See Jonathan Z. Smith, "Fences and Neighbors: Some Contours of Early Judaism," in *Imagining Religion: From Babylon to Jonestown* (Chicago Studies in the History of Judaism; Chicago: University of Chicago Press, 1982), 1–18. The polythetic classification endeavor that Smith proposes implies a polyadic understanding of religion, that is, a conception of religion as composed of many types of phenomena: material, ritual, narrative, propositional, experiential, and so forth.

6. Marshall, *Parables of War,* 37–54.

7. For an influential argument that "conflict with Jews" animates Revelation, see Adela Yarbro Collins, *Crisis and Catharsis: The Power of the Apocalypse* (Philadelphia: Westminster, 1984), 85–87. Yarbro Collins suggests that Rev 2:9 constitutes an "attack on the Jews," that "the split between Christians and Jews" has already occurred, and that John anticipates "the eventual conversion of the Jews" to Christianity. See Marshall, *Parables of War,* 122–34, for an alternate view.

8. Yarbro Collins, *Crisis and Catharsis,* 85–87, adduces only Rev 2:9, 3:9, and 11:8 to support the argument for a conflict with Jews. See Marshall, *Parables of War,* 163–73, on Rev 11.

9. See Stephen L. Dyson, "Native Revolt Patterns in the Roman Empire," *Aufstieg und Niedergang der römischen Welt* 2, no. 3 (1975): 138–75.

10. Jonathan Z. Smith, "What a Difference a Difference Makes," in *"To See Ourselves as Others See Us": Christians, Jews, and "Others" in Late Antiquity* (ed. Jacob Neusner and Ernest S. Frerichs; Chico, Calif.: Scholars Press, 1985), 3–48, at p. 47.

11. David Frankfurter, "Jews or Not? Reconstructing the "Other" in Rev 2:9 and 3:9," *HTR* 94, no. 4 (2001): 403–25.

12. Homi Bhabha, *The Location of Culture* (London: Routledge, 1994).

13. Ibid., 107: "The colonial presence is always ambivalent, split between its appearance as original and authoritative and its articulation as repetition and difference." Bhabha's strategy for a political analysis of colonialism is modeled clearly on Derrida's analysis of the duplicity that afflicts the scene of writing itself (109–10).

14. Frantz Fanon, *The Wretched of the Earth* (trans. Constance Farrington; New York: Grove Press, 1968), 39.

15. Ibid., 39, cf. 52: "When the native is confronted with the colonial order of things, he finds he is in a state of permanent tension. The settler's world is a hostile world, which spurns the native, but at the same time it is a world of which he is envious."

16. Ibid., 45–46, cf. 41: "The colonial world is a Manichean world."

17. Ibid., 52: "The colonized man will first manifest this aggressiveness which has been deposited in his bones against his own people. This is the period when niggers beat each other up, and the police and the magistrates do not know which way to turn when faced with the astonishing waves of crime in North Africa." Cf. 43: "Thus collective autodestruction in a very concrete form is one of the ways in which the native's muscular tension is set free."

18. Consider, for example, the Sepoy rebellion, whose flourishing was abetted by rumors of forced impurity through cartridges contaminated with beef and pork fat, or by flour adulterated with bone dust. Here we have in the multireligious environment of Southern Asia and also within the multitheistic territory of Hinduism an iconic action— Sepoys being forced to bite the cartridges rumored to have been greased with pork and beef fat—that corresponds illuminatingly to the bugbear of practice by devotees of Jesus in the first century: eating food offered to idols.

19. See the purity of the New Jerusalem (Rev 21:27), the role of white linen garments (Rev 19:8, 14), the purity of the holy warriors on Zion (Rev 14:4), and so forth.

20. Fanon, *The Wretched*, 54.

21. Kate Cooper, *The Virgin and the Bride: Idealized Womanhood in Late Antiquity* (Cambridge, Mass.: Harvard University Press, 1996). See also the response by Shelley Matthews, "Thinking of Thecla: Issues in Feminist Historiography," *JFSR* 17, no. 2 (2001): 39–55.

22. See Josephus, *J.W.* 6.285–300. The quote is from 6.286. I have modified the Loeb translation only by rendering ἐγκάθετοι as "deployed" rather than the Loeb's "suborned."

23. Jonathan Z. Smith, "Wisdom and Apocalyptic," in *Map Is Not Territory: Studies in the History of Religions* (Chicago: University of Chicago Press, 1978), 67–87. Smith's essay articulates some of this connection in its stress on the role of the loss of native kingship in what he terms an "apocalyptic situation."

4

"By the Finger of God": Jesus and Imperial Violence

RICHARD A. HORSLEY

Jesus was a teacher of nonviolence, even nonresistance. That was the consensus that came prominently to the fore in the late 1960s and early 1970s. This view had been important to those of us who were pacifists and/or strong believers in nonviolent direct action and counted Mahatma Gandhi and Martin Luther King among our heroes. The traditional pacifist view, however, was completely overshadowed by the vehement arguments for an apolitical as well as pacifist Jesus by prominent New Testament scholars.[1] This understanding of Jesus as a teacher of nonresistance was part and parcel of a modern Western approach to Jesus as a teacher who pronounced individual sayings such as "love your enemies," "turn the other cheek," and "do not resist (the) evil (one)."

In retrospect we can see that this view of Jesus was rooted in several interrelated assumptions and approaches of modern Western culture. On the assumption of modern individualism, Jesus was understood as an individual who taught other individuals. On the assumption that only the teachings (versus the miracles) of Jesus are reliable evidence, interpreters presented him primarily as a teacher. Following the long-established scholarly practice, codified in the chapters and verses of printed Bibles and handbooks, interpretation focused on individual sayings—purposely removed from the (supposedly) historically unreliable literary context of the Gospels. On the assumption that religion is separate from politics and economics, with Jesus categorized as religious, it was assumed that his teaching pertained to individual faith and religious ethics, not political-economic affairs. Many are now questioning those assumptions and the approach rooted in them. Jesus was almost certainly a teacher

51

whose mission was focused on groups and communities as well as individuals. As in virtually all societies prior to the modern West, moreover, religion was inseparable from political-economic life.

The vehemence with which leading scholars insisted that Jesus was a teacher of nonviolence and even apolitical nonresistance, however, cannot be explained simply as the response to a few maverick interpreters of Jesus as politically engaged, perhaps even a sympathizer with "the Zealots."[2] The 1960s and 1970s, of course, were times of national liberation movements against European and American imperial rule in the "third world," and of widespread protests against the U.S. war in Vietnam and other counterinsurgency wars. Again in retrospect, it seems like no mere coincidence that European scholars constructed an elaborate synthetic picture of "the Zealots" as a longstanding and widespread movement of violent revolt against Roman rule, as a kind of ancient Jewish "National Liberation Front."[3] As practitioners of anti-imperial violence, "the Zealots" provided a useful foil over against which Jesus could be portrayed as a sober teacher of pacifist nonresistance. It seems no mere coincidence, moreover, that New Testament scholars thus focused the issue of violence on resistance to foreign imperial rule rather than on imperial rule itself. Like many other academic fields, New Testament studies originated in late nineteenth- and early twentieth-century Germany and England during the heyday of imperialism. That Western nations were ruling and exploiting subject peoples was simply assumed as the standard order of things.[4] It was also assumed that the Gospels belonged to European Christians, whose responsibility it was to take them as authoritative Scriptures to those subject peoples. The portrayal of Jesus as a sober advocate of nonresistance in opposition to the revolutionary violence of "the Zealots' thus perpetuated the Western Christian appeal to Jesus' teaching of "love your enemy" as a device to suppress resistance to Western domination, including repressive imperial violence.

The presentation of Jesus as a teacher of nonviolence in vivid contrast with "the Zealots," moreover, perpetuated and heightened the traditional Christian stereotype of Judaism. "The Zealots" were Christian scholars' construction of the "fourth" of the principal "philosophies" or "sects" of "Judaism," who agreed basically with the teachings of the Pharisees, who were supposedly the ancestors of what became standard rabbinic Judaism. New Testament scholars' construction of "the Zealots" thus escalated into the realm of violence the deeply rooted Christian theological stereotype of Judaism as a parochial political religion, in contrast to the true individual spiritual religion of Christianity and its irenic teacher of nonresistance.[5]

It is now recognized that behind the modern scholarly construct of "the Zealots" were a variety of scribal-retainer and peasant movements of resistance that took different social forms, many of which were nonviolent.[6] The demise of "the Zealots" as a foil for interpretation of Jesus as a teacher of nonresistance should help clear the way for a closer look at the issue of Jesus and violence, particularly Jesus and imperial violence.[7] It is curious, however, that the issue of violence all but disappeared with the rise to prominence of what has been called "the third quest" during the 1990s. In studies by more liberal scholars, imperial violence and its effects on the people does not appear as a significant issue; more conservative interpreters tend to downplay imperial conquest and repressive actions in painting a more irenic setting for a focus on religious affairs.[8]

The shock of the terrorist attacks on the World Trade Center towers as symbols of global capitalism and the Pentagon as a symbol of its American military enforcer, however, brought about a sobering recognition of the contemporary realities of imperial violence and counterviolence. Americans suddenly wondered aloud, "Why do 'they' hate us so?" and many realized that Middle Eastern peoples had been asking the corresponding question for years: "Why do 'Americans' hate us so?" Meanwhile, discussion of America as an imperial superpower moved into public discourse as never before, as prominently placed "neoconservatives" insisted that the United States does indeed have an empire. And the president of the United States announced as official policy that the world's sole remaining superpower would wage preemptive war on any country that poses a threat to its security—and immediately acted on the new policy.

This is the unavoidable context in which we now return to the question of Jesus and imperial violence. The question may have a special poignancy for American Christians and biblical interpreters, moreover, insofar as Americans have, at least since the days of Thomas Jefferson, understood themselves as the new Rome as well as God's new Israel.[9] How are those of us who live in the imperial metropolis of the new Rome to deal with Jesus, who was executed as a rebel leader by the officials and military of the ancient Roman Empire?

Dealing appropriately and adequately with Jesus in his own historical context, that of the ancient Roman Empire, will require a more critical perspective on first-century politics and a more comprehensive approach than what prevailed in the context of counterinsurgency of the 1960s and 1970s and still often persists among "third questers." While the violence of imperial conquest and economic exploitation has previously often been accepted or ignored, such violence constituted the very conditions for Jesus and the movement(s) he catalyzed as well as the many contemporary Judean and Galilean movements that resisted Roman rule.[10] This is manifested most vividly in the generally accepted historical fact of Jesus' execution: by the Romans by means of crucifixion, a form of torturous execution reserved mainly for rebellious slaves and rebel leaders among subject peoples.[11] Recognition of the brutal realities of the imperial situation and its effect on the Judean, Samaritan, and Galilean peoples, moreover, opens toward the further recognition that Jesus' mission and movement(s) were fundamentally similar in most respects to other, contemporary resistance and renewal movements among the Judeans and Galileans. Contrary to the modern assumption of the separation of the religious from the political-economic, Jesus and his contemporaries dealt with spiritual power(s) as inseparable from economic subsistence and political conflict. In his/their world, political power was inseparable from spiritual power.

As important as these shifts in assumptions and perspective is a more appropriate approach to the gospel materials that provide our primary sources for the mission of Jesus, particularly Q and Mark. Investigation of the historical Jesus in general, including Jesus and violence, by focusing on isolated individual sayings is a highly problematic approach to a historical figure. An isolated saying has no meaning in itself. Meaning depends on context. Isolated individual Jesus sayings are like artifacts displayed in museum cases; they are not units of communication.

For a defensible historical inquiry, we must work from, not dispense with, the only sources that provide indications of the meaning context of Jesus' speech and action. That suggests that we work from gospel documents closest to Jesus' historical situation, such as the Gospel of Mark as a complete story and the whole series of Jesus' speeches in Q (which is not a collection of sayings but a sequence of discourses). At the very least we must work from the infrastructural components of the Gospels, such as the parallel chains of miracles in Mark and John or the parallel discourses in Mark and Q, which also provide indications of meaning context. It so happens that Mark's story and the Q series of Jesus speeches and their intermediate length components also constitute the basic units of communication about Jesus.[12]

Roman Imperial Violence, Its Effects, and Judean-Galilean Resistance

Jesus pursued his mission in a historical period framed by imperial violence against the Judean and Galilean people and their repeated struggle for independence. Imperial violence was perhaps the most important broadly determinative factor in the circumstances of his mission and the movement that he catalyzed.[13]

Roman Imperial Violence

Roman imperial violence escalated in the decades following the initial conquest by Pompey in 63 B.C.E., which was not terribly destructive. The imperial violence was regular and often brutal, as Roman armies marched in to suppress the attempts by rival Hasmoneans to retake the country and the empire-wide civil war spilled over into the recently conquered areas such as Palestine. Rival Roman warlords exploited the countryside as an economic base, with viciously enforced special levies of tribute, in order to mount their ambitious military expeditions to conquer new territories to the east. In an attempt to reestablish order in Palestine during the Roman and Judean civil war in 53–52 B.C.E., for example, the Roman warlord Cassius enslaved several thousand people in and around Magdala (Josephus, *J.W.* 1.180, seriously discounting Josephus's exaggerated figure of thirty thousand). The Romans also supplied client rulers such as the military strong-man Herod to enable them to conquer and control the people they were to rule. Galileans in particular persisted in their resistance to Herod, who had to reconquer the area three times in the three years from 40–37 B.C.E. (Josephus, *J.W.* 1.291, 303–16, 326; *Ant.* 14.295, 413–33, 450).[14]

Roman imperial violence became particularly brutal when the Romans reconquered territories after rebellions with a vengeance. The mission of Jesus was framed several decades before and after by widespread revolts of the Judean and Galilean people, which evoked extensive slaughter and destruction by the Roman armies in reconquest. At the death of Herod in 4 B.C.E., revolts erupted in every major area of the country. In a campaign that took three years, the Roman general Varus suppressed these revolts, with destruction of many villages, slaughter and enslavement of the people, and the crucifixion of thousands. Only a few miles from Nazareth, for example, the Romans burned the town of Sepphoris (and its surrounding villages?) and enslaved its inhabitants (Josephus, *J. W.* 2.68; *Ant.* 17.289). Seventy years later, after serious deterioration in both economic and political conditions, widespread revolts erupted again, in Jerusalem as well as among the villages of Judea and Galilee. The Romans again reconquered Galilee with extensive destruction, slaughter, and enslavement in about a year. In a systematic military campaign, the Romans then devastated the Judean countryside as well, and finally destroyed Jerusalem and the temple in 70 C.E. Seventy years after the great revolt, yet another massive uprising occurred in Judea, named after its messianic leader, Bar Kokhba, which the Roman armies defeated in a long and highly destructive war of attrition from 132–35 C.E. In between the revolts in 4 B.C.E. and 66–70 C.E., the Roman governors used troops to suppress swiftly protests and resistance movements that emerged periodically.

Recent studies by Roman historians are making it increasingly clear that such brutal military violence against subject peoples was standard practice by the Romans.[15] Romans believed that their own "national security" depended on the subjection of other peoples by superior military force and the extraction of "loyalty" (*fides/pistis*) and tribute from them, tribute being both a symbol of humiliation as well as a source of revenue. They were afraid that any sign of weakness such as failure to punish a revolt would invite further insurrection. In their initial conquests and again in retaliation for any rebellion, the Roman armies purposely devastated the countryside, burned villages, pillaged towns, and slaughtered and enslaved the people (Tacitus, *Ann.* 1.51, 56; 2.21; Cassius Dio 67.4.6; Augustus, *Res gest. divi Aug.*). The historian Polybius states what he believes to be the purpose: "It seems to me that they do this for the sake of terror" (10:15–17; cf. Julius Caesar, *Bell. gall.* 4.19; Cassius Dio 68.6.1–2; Pliny, *Ep.* 2.7.2).[16] More familiar to readers of the Gospels, perhaps, is crucifixion; it is certainly clear that the purpose of Roman use of the slow, torturous execution of rebels by public crucifixion in prominent places was to terrorize the surviving population into acquiescence to Roman domination (Josephus, *J. W.* 5.449–51).

The Effects of Imperial Violence

The effects of this systemic and brutal imperial violence on the people of Palestine is evident in sources such as Josephus and Roman historians. Given the limitations of an essay, I focus here only on three of the more immediate effects of the "in-your-face" imperial violence and constant threat of further violence.

First, Roman slaughter and enslavement left mass trauma among the Galileans—in the very areas where Jesus originated and carried out his mission. The memory and impact of Cassius's mass enslavement in and around Magdala (Josephus, *J.W.* 1.180) would hardly have faded by the time of Mary of Magdala and other Galileans from the area such as Cephas, Andrew, James, and John. Many villagers in the area around Nazareth may well have lost relatives and friends when the Romans burned Sepphoris and enslaved its inhabitants (Josephus, *J.W.* 2.68; *Ant.* 17.289). Similar Roman acts of terrorization would have devastated villages and towns in Judea as well, judging from Josephus's accounts of the Roman general Varus's treatment of Emmaus, another place familiar to readers of the Gospels (*Ant.* 17.291–95; cf. Luke 24:13–27). Also in Galilee, the Romans' "ethnarch" Herod Antipas extended the violent treatment of the people in his massive building projects. In the area along the Sea of Galilee just to the south of Magdala he apparently forcibly displaced a number of village communities to generate the "service" population necessary to establish his second capital city, Tiberias (*Ant.* 18.36–38).

Second, fratricidal violence erupted periodically between peoples of common Israelite heritage. Historians, social scientists, and novelists have long since recognized that subject peoples who somehow know that active resistance to repressive rule would be suicidal often turn violent in relations with other subjected peoples. The best known example in Roman Palestine is the conflict between Judeans and Samaritans. Jesus' parable of "the Good Samaritan" illustrates the underlying hostility between them. That hostility erupted most dramatically in the mid-first century when some Samaritans attacked and killed some Galileans on their way to Jerusalem for the Passover festival. In retaliation, a number of Judeans, led by the well-known brigand leader Eleazar ben Dinai, attacked some Samaritan villages. The Roman governor Cumanus finally sent out his troops, who killed many of the Judeans and captured many others, while brigand raids and local insurrections continued around the countryside (Josephus, *Ant.* 20.118–36; *J.W.* 2.232–46).

Third, imperial violence and the constant threat of more violence led to demonic possession. The subjected people somehow knew that active resistance to the imperial order would be suicidal in evoking violent Roman retaliation against their intransigence. Almost as a survival mechanism, therefore, the Galilean and Judean people focused the experience of being possessed by alien forces in the world of spirits: they were possessed by "unclean spirits" or "demons." Even at the level of scribal circles, for example the intellectual-priestly community at Qumran, Judeans came to believe that they were caught up in a world-historical struggle between maleficent superhuman spiritual forces, of Belial or Satan or the Prince of Darkness, on the one side, and God and benign spiritual forces, on the other (1QS 3–4). It has long been recognized that such beliefs in demons and the (temporary) control of history and society by Satan, unprecedented in Israelite (biblical) literature, suddenly appeared in early Roman times. There are enough hints in our sources to lead to the conclusion that demon possession was, among other things, a defensive (self-protective) response to the imperial (threat of) violence.

Judean and Galilean Resistance

In between and in some cases overlapping with their widespread revolts, the Judean and Galilean people mounted persistent resistance to their imperial and Jerusalem rulers. The most significant and sustained resistance emerged among the Judean and Galilean peasantry, while scribal circles channeled their resistance into literary production, occasional protests, and even clandestine violence.

Protests and other resistance by scribal circles were rare, presumably because of their dependence on the high priestly rulers and temple system. The temple-state, of course, had been set up as an instrument of imperial rule by the Persians, and was retained by successive imperial regimes. Once the Romans established direct rule in Judea, the Roman governors appointed and dismissed the high priests at will, virtually obliging them to collaborate in Roman imperial rule.[17] Perhaps for that very reason, many scribal circles, who had long since developed a sense of their own independent authority as the professional interpreters of Judean/Israelite cultural traditions, opposed and even condemned the priestly aristocracy as well as Roman domination.

Many of the texts produced by Judean scribal circles in the late Hasmonean and Herodian periods pronounce God's condemnation of imperial domination and Jerusalem's rulers. The tone was set by the dream-visions and surveys of history in Dan 7–12 that recount the violently oppressive treatment of Judeans by the western, Hellenistic empire(s) as far more vicious than their eastern predecessors, and anticipate the condemnation and destruction of Seleucid imperial rule in God's imminent judgment (especially Dan 7:11, 26). The Psalms of Solomon, apparently produced by a circle of intellectuals early in the Herodian period, condemn the Hasmonean rulers and particularly the Romans for their violent "trampling" of Jerusalem and anticipate that God will send the Messiah, Son of David "to destroy the unrighteous rulers/unlawful nations" (see *Pss. Sol.* 1; 2; 8; and 17, especially 17:22–24). The *Testament of Moses,* whether in its Hasmonean/Seleucid period origins or its Herodian/Roman period updating (chapters 6–7), condemns the violent oppression by both imperial and client Judean rulers and anticipates God's judgment, in which "he will come to work vengeance on the nations" (especially 6; 8; 10:3–7).

Most vivid of all are the texts from the Qumran community that had withdrawn to the wilderness, condemning the incumbent high priestly regime in Jerusalem (initially apparently the Hasmoneans) as "the Wicked Priest." Despite their withdrawal from engagement in imperial and temple-state politics, they anticipated that God would imminently mount a full-scale war, at the transhistorical heavenly level as well as the historical, against Belial/the Prince of Darkness and "the Kittim," that is, the Romans. "On the day when the Kittim fall, there shall be battle and terrible carnage before the God of Israel, for that shall be the day appointed from ancient times for the battle of destruction of the sons of darkness. . . . When the great hand of God is raised in an everlasting blow against Belial and the hosts of his kingdom . . ." (*War Scroll,* 1QM 1.9–11; 18.1–2).[18]

Certain scribal circles or teachers also mounted protests and direct resistance.[19] Again the tone was set by the earlier *maskilim* who, inspired by their own visions of God's impending judgment of the empire (in Dan 7–12), offered active nonviolent resistance to the Seleucid repression. Just before Herod died, some revered Jerusalem teachers of the law inspired their students to take down the golden Roman eagle from atop the great gates of the temple, an act of direct defiance to king and empire alike—for which Herod had them burned alive (Josephus, *J.W.* 1.648–55; *Ant.* 17.149–58). Ten years later, as the direct Roman rule by a governor was imposed, a group of intellectuals led by the teacher Judas of Gamla and the Pharisee Saddok organized the movement Josephus calls the Fourth Philosophy, insisting that their exclusive loyalty to God prohibited them from paying the tribute to Rome. A half century later, the successors of these intellectuals, frustrated at the deterioration of the imperial situation and the intransigence of the high priestly aristocracy, began assassinating prominent high priestly figures at festival times (*J.W.* 2.254–57; *Ant.* 20.186–87). These intellectual "Dagger-men" (*sicarioi*) thus launched a kind of counterterrorism to the imperial violence.[20]

The most significant resistance emerged among the Judean and Galilean peasantry. Remarkable for their nonviolent discipline were two popular protests generated by the people against provocative Roman actions that violated the most basic principles of the traditional Israelite way of life, their exclusive loyalty to God. Protesting Pilate's inflammatory introduction of troops bearing Roman army standards that displayed busts of the emperor, numbers of Judeans demonstrated against the governor's outrage, baring their throats to Pilate's soldiers' swords (Josephus, *Ant.* 18.55–59; *J.W.* 2.169–73). When the emperor Gaius ordered his bust/image to be erected in the Jerusalem temple, Galilean peasants carried out a sustained massive strike, refusing to plant their fields (*J.W.* 2.184–203; *Ant.* 2.261–88).[21]

Far more significant were the many sustained and widespread popular movements of renewal of Israelite society in resistance to domination by Rome and its local client rulers. The movements for which we have sources were of two types distinctive to the Judeans, Samaritans, and Galileans rooted in Israelite tradition.

The popular revolts in Galilee, Judea, and Perea in 4 B.C.E. and the forces led by Simon bar Giora in the great revolt in 66–70 C.E. (and the revolt led by Bar Kokhba) all took the form of messianic movements in which the people acclaimed their leader as "king."[22] Although Josephus uses the term *basileus* (king), his portrayal of these movements suggests that they were patterned after the movements of liberation from the Philistines led by Saul and especially the young David, whom their followers acclaimed as "messiah" (2 Sam 2:1–4; 5:1–4). These popular messiahs and their movements did not just assert the independent self-rule of the people, but raided the local royal fortresses and storehouses and even Roman baggage trains to "take back" the goods that had been taken from them as taxes and tribute.

In the mid-first century several other peasant movements of renewal and resistance took a different form. Prophets appearing as the new Moses and/or the new Joshua led large numbers of followers out to experience God's fantastic deliverance in the form of a new exodus and/or entry into the land or a new taking of the land from the rulers, somewhat as Joshua had shown God's victory over Jericho (Josephus, *Ant.* 18.85–87; 20.97–98, 168, 261–63; *J.W.* 2.259–63).[23] Although in their anticipation of miraculous deliverance by God the popular prophets and their movements were utterly nonviolent themselves, the Roman governors sent out sizeable military forces to suppress them.

From this survey of Judean and Galilean resistance movements and Judean scribal literature several important points stand out. First, the lines of political conflict correspond with the fundamental division between the imperial rulers and their local Herodian and high priestly clients, on the one hand, and the Judean and Galilean peasantry along with certain groups from among the scribal retainers, on the other. Second, the basic structural division involved frequent and sometimes extensive acts of military or other oppressive and repressive violence by the rulers against the subject people. Third, most popular and scribal resistance to imperial rule and violence was nonviolent, although at times of extreme crisis widespread popular revolt erupted and a few intellectuals resorted to counterterrorism when the imperial order in Judea proved utterly unresponsive to protests. Fourth, although, with the exception of Qumran literature such as the *War Scroll,* the anticipated violence does not appear in lurid images, some of the popular movements and all of the dissident scribal literature anticipated God's judgment, which involved violent destruction against the imperial rulers and their clients.

Jesus' Response to Imperial Violence

When we focus not on isolated text-fragments but on those larger historical units of communication such as Mark's story as a whole and the Q series of speeches as sources for Jesus, then his mission appears similar to other Judean and Galilean renewal movements in most significant respects, including its response to imperial violence. Jesus' mission of healing the traumatic and disintegrative effects of imperial violence can be seen particularly in his practice of exorcism understood in its historical context of Roman Palestine and in his attempt to renew village community life. The anticipation of divine counterviolence can be seen in Jesus' prophetic pronouncement of God's judgment of Roman imperial rule and rulers.

"God's Kingdom Is at Hand": Conflict and Violence in Q and Mark

In Q, a series of Jesus' speeches on key issues for the communities of his movement, Jesus as prophet enacts and gives instructions for a renewal of

Israel in its village communities over against the Jerusalem rulers and their representatives.[24] Most of the speeches deal with issues internal to the movement, such as renewal of the covenantal basis of community life (Q 6:20–49), the commissioning of envoys to extend Jesus' mission to other village communities (9:57–10:16), prayer for subsistence bread and cancellation of debts (11:2–4, 9–13), bold witnessing when hauled before the authorities (12:2–12), and anxiety about subsistence living (12:22–31).[25] Although by no means the most prominent features of the sequence of speeches, God's judgment and violence both by the rulers and by God appear at significant points. The opening prophecy by John the Baptist announces that "the coming one" will bring the fire of judgment as well as the Spirit of renewal. More ominously, the Jerusalem rulers and their Pharisaic representatives have persecuted and killed the prophets. Jesus, in response, pronounces that the Jerusalem ruling house already stands desolate under divine condemnation and that the blood of all the murdered prophets will be required of "this generation" (13:34–35; 11:39–52).

Mark's story of societal renewal is similarly pervaded by conflict. Mark's overall agenda has Jesus leading a renewal of Israel under the rule of God over against Jerusalem and Roman imperial rule.[26] Throughout the story Jesus acts and speaks in the power of God against the demonic spiritual forces and political-economic forces that are possessing and dispossessing the people. In the climactic events of the story Jesus directly confronts the Jerusalem rulers, prophetically enacting and pronouncing God's condemnation of the temple and the high priests and subtly insinuating that the people owe nothing whatever to Caesar (insofar as all things belong to God; Mark 11–12). Finally the high priests plot and take action to get rid of Jesus, turning him over to the Roman governor, who executes him as a rebel against Roman imperial rule (Mark 14–15).

Violence is operative throughout Mark's story, on both sides, as it were. On the one hand, the rulers and the demonic forces do violence to the people. Unclean spirits have possessed some of the people, touching off fratricidal social violence (Mark 5:1–20). Antipas beheads John (6:17–29). Because of the rulers' repressive violence, following Jesus will require "taking up the cross" (8:34–38). In his speech to the disciples about the immediate future, Jesus refers to war, military brutality against women and infants, and violence so pervasive that one dare not take time to get a cloak or provisions (13:3–23). Finally, in the climax of the story, the Jerusalem rulers arrest Jesus by force of arms and the Roman governor orders him beaten and executed by torturous crucifixion (14:43–15:32).

On the other hand, a counterviolence of divine judgment is operative against those demonic spirits and their leader Satan, against the Jerusalem rulers and ruling institutions, and against the Roman military forces. The Markan narrative presents this divine violence without attributing agency to God or Jesus, yet clearly indicating that God's rule is winning the struggle. Perhaps this is why we tend not to notice or discuss God's violence, although our own apologetic concern to protect the reputations of God and Jesus surely plays a role as well. The violence entailed in the victory of God's rule includes the binding of the "strong man," and the destruction of the demonic force of Legion when the "company" of pigs "charges" into the Sea (Mark 3:22–27; 5:1–13). Jesus carries out a forcible demonstration in the temple that dramatizes God's condemnation, he pronounces that the owner of the vineyard (God) will destroy the tenants (the high priestly aristocracy), and he prophesies the destruction of the temple (11:12–24; 12:1–12; 13:1–2; cf. 14:58; 15:29–30). Finally, as he expires on the cross, the curtain of the temple is torn in two, symbolizing God's judgment (15:33–39).

"My Name Is Legion": Countering Imperial Violence in the Exorcisms

It is clear particularly from key Dead Sea Scrolls produced in the Qumran community that at least some dissident Judean scribes and priests shared Jesus' and his followers' (Mark's and Q's) belief that the structural conflict and violence between Roman rulers and their subjects involved a transhistorical dimension.[27] Indeed, in the *Rule of the Community* as well as the *War Scroll,* Qumranites articulated a schematic struggle between the Prince of Light and Belial/the Prince of Darkness. This biblically unprecedented spiritual dualism was clearly a response to the concrete dualism imposed on the Judeans and Galileans by imperial violence. The priests and scribes at Qumran apparently knew that resistance was met with an escalation of imperial violence, as Josephus recounts again and again. In fact the Romans even had a dualistic ideology to match the military power they imposed on subject peoples. They understood themselves proudly as a superior civilization acting out of historic necessity to subject and maintain order over uncivilized, barbarian peoples such as the Judeans and other Middle Easterners.[28] Not surprisingly, considering the Roman imperial intransigence, the only solution that the Judean scribes and priests at Qumran could imagine was divine warfare against the foreign imperial rulers and the demonic spiritual forces in whose power they operated. The solution to imperial violence was God's violence (see especially 1QM 1–2).

The conflict between imperial violence and divine counterviolence, conceived in Mark and the Dead Sea Scrolls to operate at a transhistorical as well as a historical level, bears striking resemblance to certain cases of imperial violence and resistance by subject peoples in modern history. The Sorbonne-educated psychiatrist Frantz Fanon called the dualism he saw operative in colonial Algeria "Manichaeism."[29] The French, operating in a dualistic ideology in which they represented civilization, enlightenment, reason, and democracy, over against the irrational, violence-prone, dark-skinned people lurking in "darkness," controlled the Algerians with intransigent oppressive and repressive violence. Resident in Algeria at the beginning of the Algerian resistance, Fanon also discerned that the violence was changing direction and flowing back against the French. This may be a suggestive analogy to the way in which the scribes at Qumran fantasized their divine deliverance. Only they understood the violent confrontation to be operating at the transcendent/divine level of God versus Belial as well as the historical level of "the Kittim" (= the Romans) versus Israel, and inverted the roles and valorization of the imperial Manichaeism, the imperially subjected now being the sons of Light and the imperial armies the instruments of Darkness.

Fanon also made an astute observation about the effects of imperial violence on subject people, in his case the Algerians. Attempts to resist imperial violence with counterviolence was simply suicidal, since the French would retaliate with overwhelming power. The subject people, however, developed self-preservative mechanisms. One of the most effective was the fear of the *djinn*, or demonic spirits. The Algerians were more terrified of the djinn than of the French. This diversion of attention from the concrete cause of their oppression was quite functional, of course, since outbursts of resistance to the French would have been suicidal. Something similar was happening among the Galileans and Judeans at the time of Jesus: fear of and possession by demonic spirits, the popular ad hoc version of the dualism developed more systematically by the scholars at Qumran. This recognition of the imperial violence and the counterviolence of God's judgment in Mark and other gospel materials, combined with illumination from Fanon's astute observations of the effects of imperial violence in modern Algeria, enable us to see Jesus' exorcisms as a mode of resistance to imperial violence.

We are fairly certain that Jesus practiced exorcism, even though we judge that none of the exorcism stories provides a historically credible portrayal of an actual case. What we have are representative episodes, sorted out and developed in repeated retelling. Just as it is indefensible as historical method to analyze the sayings of Jesus in isolation, so it is also indefensible method to focus on exorcism or healing stories in isolation. As we have them, both in Mark and in the pre-Markan miracle chains, exorcism episodes were components of larger units of communication.[30] In the miracle chains, Jesus, as a popular prophet like Moses and Elijah, leads a renewal of Israel in sea-crossings, exorcisms, healings, and wilderness feedings. Both Q and Mark, which incorporates the miracle chains, expand the repertoire of the Moses- and Elijah-like prophet: he also constitutes the Twelve as representative heads of Israel undergoing renewal; sends out envoys as preachers, healers-exorcisers, and organizers of the movement; enacts covenant renewal (the speech in Q 6:20–49 and the set of dialogues in Mark 10:1–45); and pronounces God's judgment against the rulers. The exorcisms thus have meaning, not as individual acts of magic, but as manifestations of the renewal of Israel, as Jesus counteracts the effects of imperial violence.

Jesus' dramatic first exorcism leads the people of the village to recognize that he is teaching (acting) with power (*exousia*). The key to understanding the exorcism is the term *epetimesen* in Mark 1:25. "And Jesus *epetimesen* him, saying 'Be silent and come out of him!' " *Epitiman* is not the usual Hellenistic term for exorcism, and this episode in Mark is not a typical Hellenistic exorcism. It has a distinctive Palestinian Israelite meaning-context. "Rebuke" is too weak and too general a translation. The key, as Howard Kee explained some time ago, is the way *ga'ar* in Hebrew, usually translated with *epitiman* in the Septuagint, is used in the Psalms and key Dead Sea Scroll passages.[31] In the Psalms *ga'ar/epitiman* is used with parallels such as "destroy" or "vanquish" in appeals to God as Warrior coming in judgment against foreign nations or imperial regimes that conquer and despoil Israel (Pss 9:6; 28:31; 78:6; 80:16). Zechariah 3:2 is especially striking with regard to the spiritual-political dualism at Qumran and Jesus' exorcisms: "Yahweh subject (*ga'ar/epitiman*) you, O Satan!" In the Scrolls *ga'ar* occurs in the context of the struggle between God and Belial. See, for example, the *War Scroll* (1QM 14:9–11 as supplemented from 4Q491): "During all the mysteries of his [Belial's] malevolence he has not made us stray from Thy Covenant; Thou hast driven his spirits [of destruction] far from [us] (*ga'ar*), Thou hast preserved the soul of Thy redeemed [when the men] of his dominion [acted wickedly]."[32] In the dramatic first exorcism in Mark, the unclean spirit knows exactly what is happening: the holy one of God has come to destroy the demonic spirits (1:24). The spirit knows that Jesus has appeared as God's prophetic agent who, having declared that the kingdom/rule of God has come near, is now defeating the demonic forces that have possessed the people. This is narrated in language that resonates deeply with the Israelite tradition, still very much alive, of God defeating foreign imperial conquerors.

In Jesus' response to the scribes' accusation that he is possessed by Beelzebul, casting out demons by the Prince of demons, in Mark 3:22–27, and the parallel dialogue in Q 11:14–20, Jesus claims that in his exorcisms the rule of Satan is being ended as the kingdom of God is being established.

Both Jesus and his accusers assume a struggle between God and super-human forces that are beyond the comprehension of the people and impossible for the people to resist, let alone overcome.[33] This is precisely the situation of people caught in the control of imperial power, whether exercised through direct violence, or through imperial political-economic-cultural structures such as client kingship and temple-states in the ancient world or a colonial capitalist system in modern Algeria. In their self-preservative instincts, however, subjected peoples such as the Galileans and Judeans or the modern Algerians avoid suicidal resistance by under-standing their subjection to uncontrollable forces in superhuman demonic spirits. They focus not on the Romans or the French, but on the "unclean spirits" or *djinn* as the agents of their malaise and suffering.

Jesus' refutation of the accusation, however, while focused on the struggle between superhuman divine and demonic forces, has ominous political implications. "House" is a standing political metaphor for king-dom (for example, 2 Sam 7; Q/Luke 13:34). Having demonstrated that the accusation is self-contradictory, Jesus further develops the ruling-house metaphor: "No one can enter the strong man's house and plun-der his instruments (vessels) without first binding the strong man" (Mark 3:27). In the exorcisms Jesus is "plundering the strong man's instruments/tools," that is, Satan's demons. The implication is that the strong man, Satan, must have been bound—by Jesus as God's agent or more likely by God. Jesus' exorcisms are manifestations of Satan's defeat. The climax of the parallel discourse in Q 11:14–20 states the further political implication with its obvious allusion to a new exodus in which such liberating power must be from God: "Since it is by the finger of God that I cast out demons, the kingdom of God has come upon you."

That the driving out of demonic spirits at the personal-social level are manifestations of God's having defeated Satan at the controlling transcendent level—manifestations of the presence of God's kingdom—has obvious implications for the political level of the empire's rule over the people.[34]

The most dramatic and riveting exorcism Jesus performs in Mark's story (Mark 5:1–20) reveals explicitly that the struggle for deliverance and renewal of the people has ominous implications for Roman imperial domination. Possession by the "unclean spirit" causes the demoniac to be uncontrollably violent. He is driven to extreme fratricidal and self-destructive violence. The rest of the community is desperate to contain the social violence that results from possession by this superhuman alien force. But they cannot control the demoniac, even with shackles and chains, and utterly ostracize him to the fearsome world of the dead among the tombs. Immediately as he commands the unclean spirit to "come out of the man," however, Jesus elicits its name, Legion. The audience would immediately resonate with the meaning of that term: a division of Roman troops, such as those that had viciously attacked their villages, burned their houses, and slaughtered their parents or grandparents. In this episode, the possessed man is symbolic of the whole people and the demon's name identifies the Roman violence that is the concrete cause of the possessed man's violent, socially destructive behavior and the disintegration of the community.[35]

The rest of the episode is a combination of "good news," the implosion of Legion, and "bad news," the local people's dis-ease at the revelation of the demon's identity. Legion bows down before Jesus and desperately begs him not to send him/them out of the country they had taken possession of. In a sequence of military images and exodus allusions Jesus "dismisses" Legion to enter the great "troop" of swine there on the hillside, who then suddenly "charge" down the steep bank "into the Sea" and are "drowned in the Sea." In a desperate attempt to continue its occupation, Legion destroys itself. "Sea" suggest not the large inland lake between Galilee and the countryside of the Decapolis, in which the episode takes place, but the Mediterranean Sea, across which the Roman legions had come to conquer the peoples of Syria and Palestine. "Into the Sea" and "drowned in the Sea" evoke memories of the exodus of Israel, when Pharaoh's armies pursuing the Israelites had been cast "into the Sea" and "drowned in the Sea" (especially the Song of Miriam, Exod 15:1–10). Exposed and confronted by the divine power working through Jesus, imperial violence becomes self-destructive in its desperation. The events of this exorcism episode, represented as a new deliverance of Israel, like God's original deliverance from foreign imperial rule in the exodus, symbolize the political liberation of the people from Roman imperial violence.

The revelation that behind the mystification of demon-possession lay the Roman military as the real agent of their possession, however, was frightening to the community. They desperately begged Jesus to leave. It was difficult, indeed impossible, to face the real political-economic situation of imperial violence. Even though the hearers of Mark's story were hearing in this episode and others the "gospel" of God's liberation from Roman rule, they too would likely have felt uneasy and ambivalent about facing the concrete political-military forces that controlled their lives.

Our analysis of exorcism episodes in Mark and the parallel Beelzebul controversies in Mark and Q indicates that in "casting out demons" Jesus was healing the destructive effects of imperial violence. His exorcizing activity did not involve engagement in violence at the political level. Yet if we take seriously the cultural forms evident in gospel sources and the Dead Sea Scrolls, exorcizing demons meant that he was engaged in a violent struggle between God and demonic spiritual forces. Violence against self and society was the effect of possession by alien spirits. Not surprisingly, the driving out of demons was also a wrenchingly violent experience for possessed persons. Jesus' engagement, apparently as the instrument of divine power in the struggle against the superhuman demonic forces, is portrayed variously as caught up in a violent transcendent struggle. The violent demonic forces are not easily dissipated or controlled. He "vanquishes" the violent invaders of the people and he "plunders" the instruments of Satan, whom God had "bound." In the most ominous case, after driving the possessing demon out of the subjected people, his "dismissal" leads to the self-destructive implosion of "Legion," clearly symbolic of Roman imperial violence.

"Love Your Enemies": Countering the Effects of Imperial Violence in the Renewal of Village Community

Contrary to common modern assumptions, Jesus was addressing not simply individuals but groups of people in the typical contexts of agrarian society. Following the schematic account of the emergence of the "church" in the book of Acts, Christian scholars simply assumed that no coherent group of Jesus followers existed prior to the formation of the "Jerusalem community" at the outpouring of the Spirit at Pentecost. That

assumption led to the rather romanticized picture that Jesus was addressing mainly the dislocated and destitute, such as beggars, prostitutes, and
"tax-collectors and sinners." Literalist reading of a few isolated Jesus sayings resulted in the hypothesis that Jesus' first followers were a handful of
homeless vagabonds, or "itinerant radicals."[36]

Recent historical, social, and archaeological analysis has led to a more
historically precise picture of the Galilean context of Jesus' mission. The
fundamental social forms in ancient Galilee and Judea were families and
village communities comprised of a smaller or larger number of family
households. Village communities were still intact. Yet they were also
apparently disintegrating under the impact of rigorous Roman and Herodian exploitation of their principal economic resources, the products of
their peasantry.[37] The Lord's Prayer (Q 11:2–4), focused as it is on economic issues, offers evidence of the circumstances that Jesus was addressing. He and his audiences appeal to God not only for subsistence bread,
presumably because they are hungry, but also for cancellation of debts,
presumably because they have fallen seriously into debt. Jesus is thus
addressing not vagabonds who have lost their land (to debts) already and
abandoned their village communities, but people who are still struggling
for a subsistence living on their ancestral land and in their villages.

Thus, rather than catalyzing new communities, Jesus was addressing
the malaise of village communities disintegrating from the impact of
Roman and Herodian conquest and exploitation. This is evident in episode
after episode in Mark and in key speeches in Q. Mark portrays Jesus consistently as preaching and healing in villages or in village "assemblies"
(synagogai).[38] Beyond Galilee he similarly carries his mission to "the villages of Caesarea Philippi," or of the Decapolis, or the rural "regions" of
Tyre (not the cities themselves, where the ruling aristocracies resided). In
the "mission discourse" in both Mark (6:6–13) and Q (10:2–16), Jesus
sends his envoys into village communities, where they are to preach and
heal and stay and eat with particular households. In Mark (10:29–31),
Jesus, with more than a bit of hyperbole, assures those who have been sent
on mission that their households, in their village communities, will eventually be restored "a hundredfold *now in this age—houses, brothers and
sisters, mothers and children, and fields* with persecutions (italics added to
emphasize the concrete social forms and relations)."[39] Given the standard
social forms of a traditional agrarian society such as Galilee, these portrayals in Mark's story have a credible historical verisimilitude for the mission of Jesus.

Ironically, the key to how Jesus was attempting to revive and restore village communities may lie in the Q speech in which are embedded the sayings that have been used as proof-texts for Jesus' pacifism, that is, "love your enemies," "turn the other cheek," and so forth (Luke/Q 6:27–36; Matt 5:38–42, 43–48).[40] These sayings, however, can be construed to attest to nonresistance or nonviolence only if taken out of their literary and historical social contexts and read in a context constructed by modern scholars. What may have led modern interpreters to their pacifist reading of these sayings is Matthew's addition of "go the second mile," originally derived from the Roman insistence that provincials must carry a soldier's gear for one "mile." Roman soldiers had destroyed the areas of Nazareth and Capernaum, but they were not an occupying army in Galilee at the time of Jesus' mission. If we look at the *context* indicated in the *content* of the other sayings, they pertain to social-economic relations within the local community, such as borrowing or lending and insults (turn the other cheek), not interactions with outside "enemies" such as Roman soldiers. Insofar as these sayings indicate conflicts and quarreling among the people, they provide yet further evidence of the disintegration of village communities. People who have previously loaned produce to their neighbors are now desperate to be repaid to maintain their own subsistence living.

This realization leads to the important procedural point that Jesus' sayings can be understood only in their literary context, which provides virtually the only clues to their historical-social context. Those familiar with the basic covenantal texts of the Hebrew Bible (for example, Exod 20, 21–23; Lev 19; 25; Deut 15) will recognize that the set of sayings in Q 6:27–36 makes numerous allusions to covenantal teachings. A closer examination of the overall speech of Jesus in Q 6:20–49 reveals that the structuring elements are components of the Mosaic covenant, as can be discerned in texts such as Exod 20:1–17 and Josh 24.[41] It is clear from the central texts of the Qumran community, particularly the *Rule of the Community,* not only that broad covenantal patterns were still cultivated, but also that they were transformed into the fundamental, constitutive community form and ceremony of contemporary groups. By analogy with the renewed (Mosaic) covenantal community at Qumran, as evident in the *Rule of the Community,* the speech in Q 6, like the expanded version in Matt 5–7, is a renewal of covenant. In both, the center of the renewed covenant consists of covenantal teachings, principles, and/or rulings (Q 6:27–42). These are prefaced by a transformation of the blessings and curses from what had been a sanctioning promise and threat into a new declaration of God's redemption in the present, and followed by new motivating elements (the double parable of houses on rock and sand). The covenantal discourse in Q 6:20–49, moreover, is in performative speech, which means that in its performance by Jesus or subsequent "Jesus" spokespersons, speaker and audience were enacting the renewal of covenant in the community.

The sayings previously construed as teachings of nonresistance turn out, therefore, to be renewed Israelite covenantal teachings addressed to disintegrating village communities. In the sayings summarized in the saying "love your enemies, do good and lend" (Luke 6:35), Jesus exhorts people who had fallen into debilitating local conflicts to return to basic covenantal principles of mutual cooperation and care.

When the set of dialogues in Mark 10:2–45 is taken as an interrelated sequence, Jesus turns out to be delivering yet another covenantal speech at a crucial juncture in Mark's story.[42] It has been noticed long since that these episodes in Mark include several "statements of holy law," fundamental principles of social-economic-political interaction for the community. These dialogues also cite the original Mosaic covenantal principles, either individually (10:2–12) or as a set (10:17–22). While not explicitly framed as a covenant renewal speech as is Q 6:20–49, the sequence of dialogues in Mark 10:2–45 forms a covenantal speech aimed at the renewal of community life on the basis of fundamental principles grounded in the Mosaic covenant. The prohibition of divorce is apparently to reinforce the cohesion of the family unit, economic life is to follow egalitarian principles rather than imitating the exploitative practices of the wealthy and powerful, and political leadership is to be modeled on community service, not the self-aggrandizing wielding of power by imperial rulers.

"Behold Your House Is Desolate": Prophetic Pronouncement of God's Judgment

Jesus' pronouncements of God's apparently imminent judgment of the rulers are few, and their imagery subtle and restrained. Yet they are integral components of both Mark and Q, and God's judgment of the rulers appears to entail divine violence, however subtly expressed and indirectly effected. Full consideration should be taken of Jesus' declaration of divine judgment, which constitutes the framework within which he attempted to heal the effects of imperial violence and to renew Israel in its constituent village communities.

While Jesus makes several references to judgment in Q speeches directed to insiders, in two speeches he pronounces God's judgment against outsiders. The images of judgment connected with "the day of the son of man" in Q 17:22–37 evidently function as a sanction on the exhortation in all the previous speeches (cf. Q 12:8–9, in the context of 12:2–12). The image of "not peace but a sword" and the allusion to the prophecy of family division from Micah in Q 12:49–59 convey the crisis in which Jesus' proclamation and manifestation of God's kingdom has placed the people, requiring urgent action in response (cf. the woes against those who do not respond in Q 10:2–16). The speeches in 13:34–35 and 11:39–52, in contrast, announce God's judgment against the Jerusalem rulers and their Pharisaic representatives, respectively. Both of these speeches take distinctively Israelite prophetic forms, a series of prophetic woes in Q 11:39–52 and a prophetic lament that assumed divine condemnation in 13:34–35.[43] The scribes and Pharisees, and by implication their patrons in the priestly aristocracy, are charged with complicity in killing the prophets. This indictment appears to be closely related to the representation of John the Baptist and Jesus as the greatest in the line of Israelite prophets, now also martyred at the hands of the Jerusalem authorities. Although not explicitly articulated, implicit in the declaration that "the blood of all the prophets will be required of this generation" is a death sentence, according to the traditional prophetic principle that the sentence corresponds to the violent crime of the rulers.[44] The structural opposition of the people (Israel) and their rulers is more fully presupposed and articulated in the charge that counter to God's motherly care for her brood, the Jerusalem ruling house had (again) killed God's prophets sent to warn against injustice and oppression (13:34–35). And again imminent destruction by God is presupposed in Jesus' prophetic lament that the ruling house lies "desolate." God's agency is not explicitly stated, but it is clearly implied in the traditional prophetic lament form.

The Gospel of Mark also presents Jesus as pronouncing and even demonstrating God's judgment as involving violent destruction. In addition to the destruction of Roman rule and Roman army implied in the exorcism stories, Mark includes Jesus' prophetic condemnation of the temple and high priestly rulers.

The implications of these portrayals for Jesus' expectation of and indirect involvement in counterimperial violence are generally avoided by one or both of two means. First, by anachronistically reducing the Jerusalem temple to a politically innocuous religious institution and ignoring the dominant political-economic structural conflict in imperial Judea, Jesus' action in the temple is taken as a mere "cleansing."[45] Second, Jesus' prophetic declaration (and demonstration) against the temple is dismissed as mere "false witness" and/or as prophecy after the fact. The latter interpretation is secured by dating the Gospel of Mark after the Roman destruction of the temple in 70 C.E., by reading the "war and rumors of war" and "desolating sacrilege" as references to events of the great revolt of 66–70. However, once we recognize that the temple and high priesthood were not simply religious institutions, but the center of the political economy of an imperial province, it is no longer possible to pretend that Jesus' action in the temple was a "cleansing." And if interpreters recognize that Jesus and his contemporaries had been experiencing "wars and rumors of wars" and "desolating sacrileges" throughout the mid-first century at the hands of the Roman governors and military, there is no compelling reason to date the Gospel of Mark after 70 C.E. and the prophetic pronouncement against the temple as after the fact.

Mark presents Jesus' action in the temple as a forcible prophetic demonstration of God's condemnation. The citation from Jeremiah's prophetic condemnation of the (first) temple indicates that the high priests are being indicted for robbing the people of their produce (on the pretense that it is owed to God and the priests as offerings and tithes) and then fleeing into their "brigands' stronghold" for protection (they assume, hypocritically, by God). In the parable of the tenants a few episodes later (Mark 12:1–9), Jesus utters a parallel condemnation of the high priestly rulers. Jesus' forcible overturning of the tables of the money-changers—the kind of demonstration that would surely be condemned by the ecclesial, university, or political authorities today as "violent"—prefigures God's judgment of the whole temple system.

The incident of Jesus' cursing of the fig tree that frames the prophetic demonstration in the temple serves as an analogy to how the temple was to "wither away to its roots." "This mountain" that, hypothetically, would be "taken up and thrown into the sea" is clearly the Temple Mount (Mark 11:12–14, 20–24). Two episodes later, Jesus delivers the parable of the tenants, which is a prophetic declaration of how God will undoubtedly take punitive action against the high priests (12:1–12). At the end of Jesus' series of confrontations with the Jerusalem rulers, Mark has Jesus predict that "not one stone will be left upon another" in the temple complex that

Herod had constructed in grand Hellenistic style as one of the wonders of
the Roman Empire, at great cost to the Judean and Galilean people
(13:1–2). In the trial scene, Mark presents (as "false testimony") the
charge that Jesus threatened to destroy the temple and then raise it, and
then he has Jesus on the cross mocked for claiming he would destroy the
temple and rebuild it in three days (14:53–65; 15:25–32).[46] Mark's narrative thus leaves no doubt that Jesus had indeed declared a prophetic condemnation of the temple and was anticipating its destruction (see
especially the sequence in 12:38–13:2).

In Mark's narrative, moreover, Jesus' announcement of God's judgment of the temple and high priesthood is closely linked in the narrative
sequence with his declaration that the people owe no tribute to Rome
(since "the things that belong to God" include everything, nothing is left
for "the things that belong to Caesar," 12:13–17). The ensuing trial and
execution of Jesus indicate that "the high priests, elders, and scribes" collaborate with the Roman governor (to whom, according to Josephus, they
owed their positions of power).

Jesus and Imperial Violence

Roman imperial violence, in repeated military conquest and economic
exploitation, created the conditions for the emergence of Jesus and other
popular leaders as well as the conditions that they addressed. Repeated
military conquests left mass trauma in their wake, and economic
exploitation steadily undermined the traditional Israelite way of life in
Judea and Galilee, causing the disintegration of the fundamental social
forms of family and village community. According to the sequence of
speeches in Q and the overall narrative of Mark's gospel, the most substantial and important of our early sources for Jesus, he was pursuing a
renewal of Israel in resistance and opposition to Roman rule and its
client high priestly rulers. Central to his movement of resistance and
renewal were attempts to heal the effects of imperial violence, particularly possession by alien demonic spirits and the disintegration of the
fundamental form of society life, the village community. The context in
which he performed exorcisms and pressed for renewal of covenantal
mutuality and cooperation in village communities was his conviction
and proclamation that "the kingdom of God" was at hand, indeed manifested precisely in his preaching and exorcisms. That God was finally
establishing his kingdom, however, entailed the divine judgment of the

Roman military forces ("Legion") and the face of Roman rule in Jerusalem, the temple system.

In most respects, Jesus' mission resembles and stands side by side with other popular movements at the time in Judea and Galilee. He and the other popular leaders also display parallels with contemporary scribal groups and texts opposed to Roman rule and/or the high priests. Scribal texts (for example, *Psalms of Solomon*; many Dead Sea Scroll documents) and groups (e.g., Fourth Philosophy) explicitly, and popular movements, by implication, asserted that since the people (Israel) belonged directly under the kingdom of God, and Roman rulers and their Jerusalem clients stood under divine condemnation, and presumably imminent divine termination. Like the oracular prophet Jesus son of Hananiah, Jesus of Nazareth uttered prophetic laments at the imminent divine destruction of Jerusalem. Like other prophetic leaders of movements in the role of a new Moses or Joshua or Elijah, he also summoned his followers to take action in response to God's initiative in bringing about a liberation and renewal of Israel. Like the popular messiahs Anthronges (4–1 B.C.E.) and Simon bar Giora (67–70 C.E.), he was concerned with political-economic-social affairs in local communities.

With regard to the question of Jesus and violence, the historical situation is far more complicated than discerned a generation ago, and our picture must be far more nuanced. Jesus cannot be set against "Judaism" or some stereotyped Jewish group such as "the Zealots," since his mission of renewal of Israel in resistance to Roman imperial rule so closely resembles the program of other, contemporary movements. Jesus sayings previously taken out of context and used as proof-texts for pacifism and even non-resistance, such as "love your enemies," turn out to be a revival of traditional Israelite covenantal teachings directed at restoring mutuality and cooperation in village communities. Jesus was clearly not leading popular revolts, unlike the popular messiahs in 4 B.C.E. and 67–70 C.E. Yet in his prophetic demonstration and other pronouncements of God's condemnation of the temple and high priesthood, as well as in his exorcisms, he is anticipating a divine violence in judgment of the imperial violence. It appears that his program of exorcism and covenantal community renewal was based in his conviction and proclamation that, in bringing the kingdom, God was about to destroy the institutions of the imperial order.

Notes to Chapter 4

1. Oscar Cullmann, *Jesus and the Revolutionaries* (New York: Harper & Row, 1970); Martin Hengel, *Was Jesus a Revolutionist?* (Philadelphia: Fortress Press, 1971); idem, *Victory over Violence* (Philadelphia: Fortress Press, 1973).

2. For example, S. G. F. Brandon, *Jesus and the Zealots* (Manchester: Manchester University Press, 1967). Brandon, an outsider to the field, was sharply attacked by New Testament scholars.

3. Especially important was Martin Hengel, *Die Zeloten* (Leiden: Brill, 1961).

4. Recent increasing awareness of how academic disciplines originated in Western imperial culture owes much to the work of the late Edward Said, *Orientalism* (New York: Random House, 1978), and *Culture and Imperialism* (New York: Random House, 1994). Talal Asad, *Genealogies of Religion* (Baltimore, Md.: Johns Hopkins University Press, 1993), offers a critique of the distinctive understanding of religion in the West. Among a number of fine recent analyses of modern Western constructions of others' religions are Richard King, *Orientalism and Religion: Postcolonial Theory, India, and the Mystic East* (London: Routledge, 1999), and Peter van der Veer, *Imperial Encounters: Religion and Modernity in India and Britain* (Princeton, N.J.: Princeton University Press, 2001).

5. The article by John Gager in this volume incisively explores closely related aspects of this problem. In fact, there appears to be little or no reason to perpetuate the modern Western essentialist constructs of "Judaism" and "Christianity" for historical analysis and interpretation of Judean and Galilean texts and history of the first century C.E. at least up to 70 and perhaps after. In many Judean texts of the time, the term of self-identification was "Israel," with awareness of regional and historical differences, such as *Ioudaioi, Samaritanoi,* and *Galilaioi* among insiders (as in Josephus). The early gospel materials and texts of the Jesus movements, such as Q and Mark, understand themselves as within Israel (contrary to the views of earlier scholars). Even texts produced by movements loyal to Jesus (Christ) produced after the Roman destruction of Jerusalem in 70 C.E. and outside of Judea or Galilee, such as the Gospel of Matthew (Antioch) and the Apocalypse of John (western Asia Minor), still exhibit no awareness of being "Christian" versus "Jewish," and perpetuate an Israelite identity as well as Israelite tradition.

6. Richard A. Horsley with John S. Hanson, *Bandits, Prophets, and Messiahs* (Minneapolis: Winston, 1985; repr., Harrisburg, Pa.: Trinity Press International, 1999), and the series of articles behind the book that give fuller critical analysis and documentation. The great diversity of groups and movements among Judeans, Samaritans, and Galileans, along with the sharp criticism of the high priestly aristocracy and Herodian rulers in much Judean scribal literature, resists modern scholars' use of the essentialist modern concept "Judaism," particularly in its Christian theological construction. I am attempting to avoid that concept, if at all possible, and to proceed in terms of particular texts, groups, movements, and incidents, including their social location and political-religious relationships wherever evidence is available.

7. This was one of the principal issues in Richard A. Horsley, *Jesus and the Spiral of Violence: Popular Jewish Resistance in Roman Palestine* (San Francisco: Harper & Row, 1987; repr. Minneapolis: Fortress Press, 1993).

8. To take one illustration of each from significant books by valued colleagues: John Dominic Crossan's *The Historical Jesus: The Life of a Mediterranean Jewish Peasant* (San Francisco: HarperCollins, 1991), while devoting a multichapter part 2 to Judean and Galilean resistance movements (building on my earlier work), treats the Roman imperial context primarily in terms of brokerage, and violence does not appear as a significant issue in the discussion of Jesus' sayings. Paula Fredriksen's *Jesus of Nazareth, King of the Jews* (New York: Vintage, 1999), 173–84, for example, while acknowledging the imperial power relations, does not pick up on the imperial violence mentioned in the sources cited.

9. Anders Stephanson, *Manifest Destiny: American Expansion and the Empire of Right* (New York: Hill & Wang, 1995).

10. See Horsley, *Jesus and the Spiral of Violence*, chapters 1–2. Roman imperial conquest and rule is receiving increasing critical attention in recent books, such as Warren Carter, *Matthew and Empire: Initial Explorations* (Harrisburg, Pa.: Trinity Press International, 2002).

11. Martin Hengel, *Crucifixion in the Ancient World and the Folly of the Message of the Cross* (Philadelphia: Fortress Press, 1977); E. P. Sanders, *Jesus and Judaism* (Philadelphia: Fortress Press, 1985), 294–322.

12. The problems inherent in standard approaches to the use of sources in constructing "the historical Jesus" are in need of searching criticism. Some key aspects of the problems have been identified in critical responses to some studies, such as Crossan, *Historical Jesus*. While working toward a more substantial study of these problems, and in searching for a more defensible historical approach, I have made some provisional suggestions in *Jesus and Empire: The Kingdom of God and the New World Disorder* (Minneapolis: Fortress Press, 2003), chapter 3.

13. The next several paragraphs provide a brief summary of longer recent accounts. My own most recent is in *Jesus and Empire*, chapters 1–2, with references to primary texts and secondary literature.

14. See further the critical analysis and discussion in Richard A. Horsley, *Galilee: History, Politics, People* (Valley Forge, Pa.: Trinity Press International, 1995), 54–56.

15. The following paragraphs are heavily dependent on such recent studies: Susan Mattern, *Rome and the Enemy: Imperial Strategy in the Principate* (Berkeley: University of California Press, 1999); J. E. Lendon, *Empire of Honor* (Oxford: Oxford University Press, 1997); Claude Nicolet, *Space, Geography, and Politics in the Early Roman Empire* (Ann Arbor: University of Michigan Press, 1991); William V. Harris, *War and Imperialism in Republican Rome, 327–70 B.C.* (Oxford: Oxford University Press, 1979); Keith Hopkins, *Conquerors and Slaves: Sociological Studies in Roman History* (Cambridge: Cambridge University Press, 1978).

16. "The aim was to punish and to terrify. . . . It was traditional; it was the Roman way." Mattern, *Rome and the Enemy*, 115–22. See also E. L. Wheeler, "Methodological

Limits and the Mirage of Roman Strategy," *Journal of Military History* 57 (1993): 35–36.

17. On the temple-state as an instrument of imperial rule, see Jon Berquist, *Judaism in Persia's Shadow: A Social and Historical Approach* (Minneapolis: Fortress Press, 1995); Joachim Shaper, "The Jerusalem Temple as an Instrument of the Achaemenid Fiscal Administration," *Vetus Testamentum* 45, no. 4 (1995): 528–39. On the collaboration of high priests in Roman imperial rule, see Richard A. Horsley, "The High Priests and Politics of Roman Palestine," *JSJ* 17 (1986): 23–55; and Martin Goodman, *The Ruling Class of Judea* (Cambridge: Cambridge University Press, 1987).

18. Translation from Geza Vermes, *The Dead Sea Scrolls in English* (London: Penguin, 1997).

19. For further analysis of such scribal-retainer movements, see Horsley, *Jesus and the Spiral of Violence,* chapter 3.

20. See further Richard A. Horsley, "The Sicarii: Ancient Jewish Terrorists," *JR* 59 (1979): 435–58.

21. Fuller analysis of these and other popular protests can be found in Horsley, *Jesus and the Spiral of Violence,* 99–120.

22. Documentation and critical analysis in Richard A. Horsley, "Popular Messianic Movements around the Time of Jesus," *CBQ* 46 (1984): 471–93.

23. Documentation and critical analysis in Richard A. Horsley, "'Like One of the Prophets of Old': Two Types of Popular Prophets at the Time of Jesus," *CBQ* 47 (1985): 435–63.

24. Laid out with extensive critical analysis and argument in Richard A. Horsley and Jonathan A. Draper, *Whoever Hears You Hears Me: Prophets, Performance, and Tradition in Q* (Harrisburg, Pa.: Trinity Press International, 1999).

25. These speeches contain many of the sayings that Jesus scholars following the standard analysis of separate individual sayings judge to be "authentic" or "early," as can be seen in such works as Crossan, *Historical Jesus.* By isolating such sayings from their literary context in Jesus' speeches in Q, however, we forfeit the only guide we have to their early meaning-context in the interaction between Jesus and his followers.

26. An extended argument that the dominant plot in Mark's gospel is not focused on discipleship but on Jesus' renewal of Israel over against the Roman and Jerusalem rulers is given in Richard A. Horsley, *Hearing the Whole Story: The Politics of Plot in Mark's Gospel* (Louisville, Ky.: Westminster/John Knox, 2001), chapters 4–5.

27. I am purposely avoiding the term "apocalyptic/apocalypticism." As a highly synthetic modern scholarly construct based on motifs abstracted from a wide-ranging selection of Judean and other texts, it often does not fit particular texts and movements very well, and imports features that may not be inherent to particular texts. It simply cannot be assumed that popular Judean, Samaritan, and Galilean messianic or prophetic movements shared the same ideas and motifs that are found in Judean apocalyptic literature such as Daniel, *1 Enoch,* and the *Assumption of Moses.* See the critical reflections in Horsley, *Jesus and the Spiral of Violence,* 129–46. With regard to treatment of "the historical Jesus," liberal interpreters oppose and conservative interpreters defend features of

"apocalypticism" that are not obviously rooted or indicated in gospel texts. For the sake of more precise historical understanding, the fields of New Testament studies and Jewish history in late Second Temple times need a critical deconstruction of the "apocalypticism" construct. I have attempted some provisional rethinking of the construct in connection with early gospel materials in "The Kingdom of God and the Renewal of Israel: Synoptic Gospels, Jesus Movements, and Apocalypticism," in *The Origins of Apocalypticism in Judaism and Christianity* (vol. 1 of *The Encyclopedia of Apocalypticism*; ed. John J. Collins; New York: Continuum, 2000), 303–44; and Horsley, *Hearing the Whole Story*, 121–36.

28. References and discussion in J. P. V. D. Balsdon, *Romans and Aliens* (Chapel Hill: University of North Carolina Press, 1979), especially 30–70; and Mattern, *Rome and the Enemy*, especially 66–80.

29. See particularly Frantz Fanon, *The Wretched of the Earth* (1961; repr., New York: Grove Press, 1968). Fanon was vilified in the United States for advocating anti-colonial violence. His principal argument, however, was that the violence imposed by European colonialism on the Algerians was now "changing direction," as it flowed back against the French in the Algerian revolt. Fanon's analysis was applied to Jesus' exorcisms in print first by Paul W. Hollenbach, "Jesus, Demoniacs, and Public Authorities: A Socio-Historical Study," *JAAR* 49 (1981): 567–88. I have explored the application further in *Hearing the Whole Story*, 141–48.

30. Burton L. Mack, *A Myth of Innocence: Mark and Christian Origins* (Philadelphia: Fortress Press, 1988), chapter 8, provides an instructive discussion of previous scholarship on the miracle chains.

31. Howard Clark Kee, "The Terminology of Mark's Exorcism Stories," *NTS* 14 (1968): 232–46.

32. Translation from Vermes, *The Dead Sea Scrolls in English*, 178.

33. Analysis here depends on my earlier attempt to understand demon possession and exorcism in *Jesus and the Spiral of Violence*, 184–90, and a more recent attempt in *Hearing the Whole Story*, 139–48.

34. For more developed analysis, see Horsley, *Jesus and the Spiral of Violence*, 184–90, and Crossan, *Historical Jesus*, 313–20.

35. Crossan, *Historical Jesus*, 315, refers to a striking comparative case among the Luvale people where those who suffer from *bindele*, the word for "European," were believed to be possessed by the spirit of (a) European; found in Barrie Reynolds, *Magic, Divination, and Witchcraft among the Barotse of Northern Rhodesia* (Berkeley: University of California Press, 1963), 133–35.

36. Gerd Theissen, *The Sociology of Early Palestinian Christianity* (Philadelphia: Fortress Press, 1978); with criticism in John K. Elliott, "Social Scientific Criticism of the New Testament and Its Social World," *Semeia* 35 (1986): 1–33; Horsley, *Sociology and the Jesus Movement* (New York: Crossroad, 1989), chapters 1–3. Sayings such as "hate father and mother" or "leave the dead to bury the dead" are hyperbole about the extreme urgency of following Jesus or responding to his mission, and are not to be taken literally. For a criticism of the "tax collectors and sinners" view of Jesus' audience, see Horsley, *Jesus and the Spiral of Violence*, 209–31.

37. This is the conclusion of the analyses of evidence for land-tenure village economic life in Horsley, *Galilee,* chapters 8–9.

38. That the *synagogai* in Mark's gospel refer to village assemblies rather than religious buildings is argued with a variety of references in Horsley, *Galilee,* chapter 10.

39. This understanding of Mark 10:31 originated with several students from Burma, Nicaragua, and the Philippines who had direct experience of peasant village life, in a course at Harvard Divinity School, fall term, 1990.

40. The following interpretation of the "love your enemies" set of sayings is more fully developed in Horsley, *Jesus and the Spiral of Violence,* 259–73.

41. For much further development of the interpretation of Q 6 as covenant renewal, see Horsley and Draper, *Whoever Hears You Hears Me,* chapter 9.

42. See further, Horsley, *Hearing the Whole Story,* 186–94.

43. These passages are more fully analyzed in Horsley and Draper, *Whoever Hears You Hears Me,* chapter 13.

44. Just as those condemned in Israelite prophetic oracles may seem indefinite, yet can be discerned from the indictment of the rulers or their officers in the immediate context, so also in Q 11:39–52 the indictment of the Pharisees in the woes in 11:39–48 indicates who stands condemned in "this generation/this kind" in 11:49–51.

45. This often has a Christian supersessionist dimension as well, the "cleansing" supposedly done to prepare the temple for Gentile Christians.

46. This evidence is further confirmed by the way the Gospel of John blunts Jesus' action and declaration about the destruction and rebuilding of the temple (John 2) by making it refer to the death and resurrection of his body.

5

Constructions of Violence and Identities in Matthew's Gospel

WARREN CARTER

Discussions of violence in Matthew have concentrated on two areas, namely the death of Jesus and the persecution of Jesus' disciples. Christian scholarly discussion has conventionally attributed both acts of physical violence to the Jews.

Several recent studies, though, suggest that these often asserted claims of Jewish violence need reexamination. In relation to claims of Jewish responsibility for Jesus' violent death, I have argued previously that the conventional de-politicized and de-Pilatized analysis of Jesus' death is only possible when scholars either ignore or misrepresent the power dynamics of the imperial situation that Matthew's text assumes and critiques: namely, the sociopolitical roles of the ruling Jerusalem elite; the alliance between this local elite and Pilate; the use of Roman justice to maintain Roman elite interests; the enormous power of Pilate, the provincial governor, to uphold elite interests; the sociopolitical significance of crucifixion; and the text's astute disclosure of Pilate's governing tactics, to name but six.[1]

The claims of Jewish violence against disciples of Jesus are more difficult. Such claims are usually made on the basis of a transparent reading: if the text says it, it must be so. Shelly Matthews, though, questions the presumption of this unreflective "prooftexting" (her term) and the ready binaries (Jew/persecutor; Christian/persecuted) that mark its discussion.[2] She urges a recognition of the theological, literary, and psychological factors shaping the gospel[3] in order to counter "positivistic interpretive procedures" that assume texts are transparently referential.[4]

Matthews' arguments raise issues that need more consideration than is possible here. For example, in recognizing the invested and perspectival nature of the New Testament texts, can the historical accuracy of the numerous New Testament references to Jewish violence be subsumed by theological, literary, and psychological factors? Might not the lack of sources outside the New Testament be explained by the marginal social location of the early Christian movement relative to the grander scheme of things? Moreover, a volume edited by Catherine Wessinger features at least four case studies involving millennialist groups that were violently assaulted by ruling authorities in situations where the millennialist group did not initiate the violence, was not committed to violence, but was perceived as a threat to societal order.[5] That is, the conventional scenario of the gospel's millennialist audience as the recipients of persecution is, sociologically, not implausible. While identifying much intra-Jewish violence (exacerbated by imperial oppression), Josephus records violence against Jews around 70 C.E. in Antioch, a possible location for Matthew's community (*J.W.* 7.46–74, 100–11). Did these outbreaks of violence include violence against Jesus' followers as followers by Jews and/or by Gentiles? That is possible, but plausibility of course is not certainty.

Both areas of inquiry raise questions about the current scholarly presumption that Matthew depicts violence along ethnic (Jewish) lines, suggesting that fresh attention to the construction of violence in Matthew's gospel is required. Two questions will guide this inquiry. How does Matthew construct violence? And how does that construction function? The double question recognizes that language has both representational and performative qualities. In its particular contexts, language "entexts" ways of thinking about and being in the world, commends a worldview while contesting others, inscribes conflict and scenarios of resolution, and constructs group identities with boundaries that embrace and exclude.[6] How, then, does Matthew's gospel construct violence? What role does violence play in the various overlapping and intertwined identities that the gospel constructs—for followers of Jesus, nonfollowers of Jesus, Jew, Gentile, elite, nonelite, male, female? In what understandings and experiences of life do such representations of violence make sense, and make sense of what?

Scholarly Constructions of Violent Matthean Jews

I have framed questions above in terms of what *the gospel* or *Matthew* constructs. But perhaps it would be more accurate to reframe them in terms of what *interpreters* construct. For instance, five texts are commonly cited to support claims that Jews commit violence against disciples and that Matthew presents Jewish violence against followers of Jesus as pervasive, necessary, and predictable: the beatitude about persecution (5:11–12), disciples in mission (10:21), the parable of the tenants (21:33–45), the condemnation of the scribes and Pharisees (23:34), and the lament over Jerusalem (23:37–39).[7] But the citation of these texts to sustain claims of Jewish violence against Jesus' followers is problematic on at least three counts. Interpreters overlook the absence of the explicit subject "Jews" in any of the texts, ignore the fact that there is usually nothing ethnically specific about the posited scenarios, and problematically generalize the characteristics of a subgroup defined by societal status to a whole people defined by ethnicity. That is, Matthean scholars have often expressed their observations in ethnic terms when categories of societal status would be much more appropriate.

For example, in 5:11, "Blessed are you when they revile and persecute you," the third person plural subject of the verbs "revile" and "persecute" is not explicitly identified. Who constitutes the "they"? Scholars, trained to think primarily in ethnic categories, commonly assume and supply "Jews," but there is nothing ethnically specific about the situation (cf. 10:17–18). Indeed, attention to the wider context of the beatitudes suggests societal status is paramount in this passage. The beatitudes' broad terms ("the poor in spirit," "the meek," "those who hunger and thirst for justice") suggest generic scenarios based on structures of power involving exploitation and oppression by elites.[8] Contextual (4:17–25) and intertextual clues (the metonymic evoking of Isa 61 and Ps 37 [LXX 36] in 5:3–6[9]) indicate situations of inequitable social relationships and vast material poverty. Hence explicating the subject of the verbs in 5:11 as "Jews" misleadingly highlights ethnicity (how to identify those being oppressed?) and ignores the pervasive sociopolitical realities of power in imperial/agrarian economies. Elite groups, of course, include Jewish elites, but societal status, much more than ethnicity, is foregrounded.

The chapter 10 references, while located in Jesus' instructions to his disciples to undertake mission only in Israel (10:5–6), extend far beyond this literary fiction. Verses 17–18 describe violent opposition from elites, both Jewish (councils and synagogues) and Gentile (governors and kings). The instructions identify the violent way that elites regardless of ethnicity defend the status quo against the disciples' mission.[10] Verse 21 depicts household violence even to death, brother against brother, father against child, children against parents.[11] In verses 34–36, these household divisions are universalized as Jesus describes his mission "on earth." He goes on to expand the household divisions under the general rubric, "one's foes will be members of one's own household." The ten subsequent constructions in verses 37–42 concerning response to his mission, translated appropriately in the NRSV by "whoever,"[12] do not designate a specifically ethnic focus. The point is confirmed by 10:22, "you will be hated by all" (ὑπὸ πάντων).

The parable of the tenant farmers (21:33–45) who beat and kill the rent collectors has also been misinterpreted as a condemnation of Israel for violence against God's messengers.[13] But 21:45–46 indicates that the parable is directed against Jewish elites. To designate the violent actors as "Jews" misapplies a general ethnic category to a subgroup, and arbitrarily elevates ethnicity over societal status and role. The latter are emphasized by the parable's scene and the interpretive comment of 21:45.

The fourth text, 23:34 ("Therefore I send you prophets, sages, and scribes, some of whom you will kill and crucify, and flog . . . , and pursue . . ."), does specify a referent. It is part of a "woe" addressed to the elite "scribes and Pharisees" (23:13, 15, 23, 25, 27, 29), who have been characterized previously as members of the powerful Jewish leadership (2:4; 5:20; 15:1; 27:62).[14] The text condemns some Jews, but not all Jews, as violent murderers of "prophets and wise men and scribes" (23:34). Jesus' violent rhetoric is directed against a particular group constituted by its powerful social status and function. This group, of course, comprises Jews, but to designate its violence as "Jewish" arbitrarily overlooks social status and gender, and inappropriately turns the violence of a few into a general ethnic characteristic.

Similar issues are involved in interpreting the term "Jerusalem" in the fifth text, 23:37–39. Commonly, Jesus' condemnation of Jerusalem for rejecting prophets is read as a condemnation of all Jews. But previously, the gospel has especially constructed Jerusalem as the city of the elite (2:3–4; 15:1) that violently resists God's purposes (2:3–4, 16–18; 16:21; 20:16–18; chapters 26–27) and against whose leadership Jesus has announced judgment (21:12–13, 18–19, 41–43, 45; 22:7).[15] Part of the leadership group, the scribes and Pharisees (cf. 2:4; 27:62), has been the object of similar condemnation throughout chapter 23. In presenting Jerusalem in these terms, the gospel is consistent with a thread that runs through the traditions concerning the violent rejection of prophets. While these traditions speak of the people's rejection of prophets,[16] they also frequently present prophets as victims of resistant, often violent, acts by elite figures (kings, queens, priests, officials, and so forth).[17] Matthew 23:27 targets an elite, male, Jewish group for which the unmodified term "Jews" is an inappropriate interpretive category.

Also overlooked by these unnuanced Christian scholarly claims of pervasive Jewish violence in Matthew's gospel is the observation that the generic term "Jews" (Ἰουδαῖοι) does not appear as the subject for any verbs denoting acts of violence. Matthew uses Ἰουδαῖοι five times: four times to refer to Jesus as king of the *Ioudaioi* in the birth (2:2) and passion narratives (27:11, 29, 37); and once in 28:15 to refer to the report of Jesus' disciples stealing his body that circulates "among the *Ioudaioi* to this day." In all five instances the *Ioudaioi* have no active, let alone violent, role. In four of the references they are the projected subjects of Jesus' rule, and in one reference the object of the elite's information spin and bribes. The gospel does not construct violence around the term *Ioudaioi*.

Nor does the noun "Israel" in any of its twelve uses identify Israel as an agent of violence.[18] That is, violence, and there is plenty of it in the gospel, is not identified with this ethnic group.

The brief discussion of these five central texts and of the terms *Ioudaioi* and "Israel" indicates both the active role *interpreters* play in constructing violence in Matthew along ethnic lines, and the apparent reluctance of the gospel to do so.

Definition

How, then, does the gospel construct violence and to what end? To assist in answering these questions, and without claiming an exhaustive list, I have attempted to catalogue the gospel's references to violence on the accompanying table in ten categories, according to the agents, type, and objects of the violence.

Classification of References to Violence in Matthew (not exhaustive) by Agents

Agents of Violence	References	Types of Violence	Object
1. Elite (Specified)			
Herod and Jerusalem elite	2:7–23	Death	Bethlehem infants
Pharisees	9:34; 12:24	Verbal violence: demonizing Jesus	Jesus
Synagogue leaders	10:17	Flogging	Disciples
Kings/governors	10:18	Legal; dragged	Disciples
Pharisees/synagogue	12:14	Death	Jesus
Herod Antipas; Herodias	14:1–12	Death	John the Baptist
Jerusalem leaders (elders, chief priests, scribes)	16:21	Suffer, death	Jesus
Jerusalem leaders	17:22–23	Death	Jesus
Rome	17:24–27	Tax	Jewish disciples
Jerusalem leaders (chief priests, scribes)	20:18	Death	Jesus
Gentiles = Roman governor	20:19	Mock, scourge, crucify	Jesus
Vineyard tenants (Jerusalem elite: elders, chief priests, Pharisees, 21:23, 45)	21:33–46	Beating, killing, stoning slaves	Slaves, prophets, Jesus
King's allies; Jerusalem elite (21:45; 22:15)	22:1–10, esp. 22:6	Shameful treatment; killing slaves	Slaves, prophets; disciples
Scribes and Pharisees	23:34	Death; scourge, persecute	Prophets, wise ones, scribes
Jerusalem	23:37–39	Kill; stone	Prophets; those sent
Jerusalem elite (chief priests; elders, 26:3,14, 47, 57–68; 27:1–2)	Chs. 26–27	Crucifixion	Jesus
Roman governor Pilate	27	Whipping; crucifixion	Jesus
Roman soldiers	27:27–31	Mocking; striking; stripping; spitting	Jesus

2. Elite: Implicit

Elite	5:10–12	Persecute; revile; speak evil falsely	Disciples
"They"	10:17a	Hand over to councils	Disciples
"They"	11:18	Rhetorical: demonization	John the Baptist

3. Imperial Powers and Structural Violence Evoked and Condemned

Babylon	1:11–12	Military, political, sociopolitical control	Israel
Assyria (intertextual links)	1:23; 4:15–16	Military, political, sociopolitical control	Israel
Rome	5:41	*Aggareia:* forced labor	Disciples
Rome and Jerusalem allies	9:36	Harassed and helpless	Nonelite Israel
Rome and Jerusalem allies	11:28–30	Laboring and heavy laden	Nonelite
Rome and Jerusalem allies	Chs. 8–9; 15:29–31, etc.	Illness	Nonelite
Rome and Jerusalem allies	14:13–21 15:32–39	Illness	Nonelite
Imperial rulers/elite in parables	13:24–30	Economic sabotage	Elites in competition
	18:23–34	Economic	Retainers/slaves
	18:34	Torture, judicial	Slaves
	20:1–16	Economic	Nonelites
	21:33–45	Physical, death, beating and killing slaves	Slaves/elite allies
	22:1–10	Physical Destruction of city	Slaves Elite allies
	24:51	Physical	Slaves
Imperial rulers/elite in parables: slave-on-slave violence	18:28–30 24:48–49	Physical, judicial Physical	Slaves Slaves
Rome; the way of all empires	20:25–28	Hierarchical, dominating rule	Elite
Jerusalem temple	21:12–17	Economic, political, religious control	Jerusalem elite

Male treatment of women; patriarchal marriage/ divorce practices	5:27–30, 31–32; 19:3	Gender discrimination	Males; elites
Wealth	19:16–22	Economic exploitation	Male elite
Rome and Jerusalem elite (chief priests, Pharisees, Pilate)	27:62–66; 28:11–15	Imperial control and spin	Nonelite
Nations	24:6–8	Wars, famine	Nations, people
Barabbas (?)	27:15–18; cf. 5:39–41	"Notorious prisoner" —violent opponent of elite?	Elite?

4. Synagogues

Councils	10:17	Flog	Disciples
Leaders (scribes and Pharisees)	23:34	Flog	Disciples

5. Crowds

great crowd . . . from the chief priest and elders	26:47	Physical (with swords and clubs)	Jesus
Jerusalem crowd	27:15, 20, 24	Rhetorical; collusion in death	Jesus

6. Towns

	10:14, 23	Persecute	Disciples

7. Households

On earth (10:34)	10:21–22, 28 (?), 34–36	Relational betrayal; kill opposition	Disciples—by siblings and children

8. Disciples

Tempted disciples	18:8a, 9a	Physical	Self, tempted disciples
Judas	26:47–50	Relational	Jesus
Judas	27:3–10	Physical	Judas
One who was with Jesus (?)	26:51	Physical	Slave of high priest
Peter	26:69–75	Relational	Jesus

9. Satan

The devil	13:19, 28, 38–39	Snatches away gospel; sabotages and destroys God's work	Disciples; world; God
Devil's agents: empires; human agents	4:8; 13:28, 38	Structural	Nonelite; God

Devil's agents: demons	8:28–34, etc.	Physical; socioeconomic, political	2 demoniacs; herd of swine
10. Jesus and God	8:12	Eschatological condemnation	"Children of the kingdom"
	8:16; 9:33, 38, etc.	ἐκβάλλω; throw out/ exorcize demons	People possessed by demons
	10:15 10:34,	Eschat. condemn. Eschat. condemn. etc. sword	Rejecting towns On earth; households
	11:20–24	Eschat. destruct.	Chorazin; Bethsaida; Capernaum
	9:4; 12:34; 16:1; 19:3	Rhetorical— demonization (4:1, 3; 6:13; 13:38)	Scribes, Pharisees, Sadducees (elite)
	13:40–42 13:49–50	Eschat. destruct. Eschat. destruct.	"All causes of sin" and doers of lawlessness; evil ones
	15:7, 12–14	Rhetorical	Pharisees & scribes from Jerusalem
	15:26	Rhetorical	Canaanite woman
	16:23	Rhetorical— demonization	Peter
	18:6	Eschat. destruct., drowning	Any who causes a believer to sin
	18:8–9 5:29–30	Eschat. destruct.	Sinning disciples
	18:35	Eschat. destruct.	Slaves/unforgiving disciples
	21:12–22	Judgment on temple	Jerusalem elite
	21:23–22:14	Judgment	Jerusalem elite
	22:11–14	Judgment	Disciples
	Ch. 23	Rhetorical	Scribes and Pharisees
	Ch. 24:1–2	Judgment	Temple
	24:27–31	Jesus' *parousia* (military; cosmic)	Roman power (eagles); all contrary to God's purposes

	24:36–25:10 (3 parables)	Jesus' *parousia*	Slaves/those not ready, watchful
	25:31–46	Judgment	All people
11. Sundry Enemies of God and Disciples			
Various enemies	5:39–44	Physical, socioeconomic, political	Disciples
People of violence	11:12	Not specified	God's empire
Unspecified persecutor	13:21	Unspecified person	Disciples
Nations/all	10:22; 24:9	Hate; tribulation; death	Disciples

Before I discuss the table's contents in detail, it is necessary to address the issue that constructing the table immediately raises, the problem of defining violence.[19]

The extensive literature on violence in general, and religious violence in particular, faces a similar problem of definition.[20] The old cliché concerning beauty and pornography ("I know it when I see it") may be apt. The discussion is complex, diverse, and invested. Violence often exists or does not exist in the eye of the politically committed beholder.

C. A. J. Coady identifies three approaches to defining violence.[21] The first provides what Coady calls a "restricted" definition that depicts violence in terms of the interpersonal infliction of physical injury. The *Oxford English Dictionary* entry typifies this approach: violence is "the exercise of physical force so as to inflict injury or damage to persons or property." The second approach, called a "wide" definition, extends this definition in two ways: (1) beyond the physical to other forms of violence such as psychological and rhetorical violence, and (2) beyond the interpersonal to structural/systemic and societal dimensions, to matters that are often engaged under the heading of "social justice." "Wide" definitions emphasize inflicting harm by any means[22] (including by laws, policies, institutions, and so on), and/or diminishing a person's choices, possibilities, and access to resources.[23] The third approach discusses violence in terms of its legitimacy, namely violence is the illegal and illegitimate use of force.[24]

While discussions of violence often employ one of these categories, I will argue that for Matthew's gospel aspects of all three definitions—the interpersonal and the structural, the physical and rhetorical/pyschological, the legitimate (God's, Jesus') and illegitimate (the present social structure)—are necessary to establish a framework adequate for describing the gospel's construction of violence.

Definition affects what is included in the table in several ways.

- Consonant with the wide definition, the chart includes verbal or rhetorical violence along with physical violence.
- Also consonant with the wide definition, the chart indicates extensive attention to the role of elites. I will elaborate this larger context of societal or structural violence presently.
- A further consequence of a wide definition means including what John Galtung calls "cultural violence," the use of "the symbolic sphere" of human existence such as religion to identify God as an agent of violence (category 10).[25]
- A fourth issue concerns the categorization of some of the references with unspecified subjects. I have included 5:10–12 in the second category of "Elite: Implicit" because I read the beatitudes as involving a material struggle against elite domination and injustice. The first two beatitudes echo the Sabbath/Jubilee tradition of Isa 61:1–2,[26] and the third beatitude in 5:5 ("blessed are the meek for they shall inherit the earth") quotes Ps 37:11, 22, 29 (LXX 36), metonymically evoking biblical traditions that speak about God's salvation of the suffering poor from the injustice imposed by oppressive elites.[27] I have similarly located 10:17a ("they will hand you over to councils") in this second category. Who are the "they" who will do the handing over? Are they authorized agents of the powerful named in 10:17–18, or are they "any person" who exercises initiative? While their identity is not clear, their initiative and complicity in the subsequent violent actions of the elite (synagogue authorities, governors, and kings) is at least arguable. Also problematic is 10:34–36. According to the restricted definition, these verses about household foes would seem not to belong on the list because, while they designate opponents, they do not specify physical violence. But for contextual reasons I have grouped them in the seventh category ("Households") with, and taken them as an elaboration of, the very violent household animosity in 10:21 in which members of the household bring about the death of disciples. Likewise I have included the reference in 10:28 to killing the body with

these household scenarios, though given that 10:17–18 is part of the context, perhaps it should not be restricted to households alone.

Violence by Ruling Elites

Violence by elites dominates the table (table: categories 1–4). Toward Jesus, they are rhetorically (9:34; 12:24) and physically violent, mocking, flogging, crucifying, and killing him (16:21; 17:22–23; 20:18–19; chapters 26–27). They are violent toward their own people (2:16–18), John (14:1–12), and disciples (10:17–18). This violence includes physical killing (the Herods in chapters 2 and 14), predictions of crucifying, flogging, and pursuit (10:17–18; 23:34[28]), and verbal violence (reviling, speaking evil falsely, 5:10–12).[29]

Who are the elite and why employ language of sociopolitical status rather than ethnicity? The elite comprises, as is typical in an imperial society, the leadership people, an alliance of Gentiles (kings, governors, Pilate) and Jews (the Jerusalem elite: chief priests, Pharisees and scribes,[30] synagogue authorities, and so forth). While the category embraces both Jew and Gentile, models of imperial societies[31] and Matthean usage prohibit any attempt to subdivide on ethnic grounds. Matthew 10:17–18 holds together violence against disciples from synagogues (flogging ordered by leaders)[32] with seizure and trials before governors and kings. The passion prediction in 20:18–19 identifies violent roles for both the Jerusalem elite and the Gentiles (= Romans); the former condemn Jesus to death while the latter mock, flog, and crucify him. Consequently and consistently, the passion narrative features the alliance of Jerusalem and Roman elites in removing Jesus. Such alliances are typical of Rome's imperial strategies and, in relation to interpreting the Gospels, have been too readily overlooked by New Testament scholars.[33]

Nor can we subdivide this elite grouping into secular and religious groups, as is often done (the ubiquitous "religious leaders" in Matthean studies).[34] Rather, as is typical in imperial worlds, the Jerusalem elite intertwines sociopolitical, economic, and religious power.[35] Priests, scribes, and Pharisees are constructed as political figures (2:4; 27:62–66). In this regard, I should emphasize that I am reading the parables of chapters 21–22 with their repeated references to killing God's messengers, prophets, and the son in relation to and directed particularly against this Jerusalem elite (so 21:23, 45; 22:15), not against all Israel or all Jews. That is, scholars who talk of the salvation history of "Israel/the Jews" as rejection of and by God do so without the nuancing that both the text and the imperial context require.[36]

Elite violence against Jesus exemplifies aspects of the restrictive definition of violence mentioned above. Employing the wide definition, though, I would argue that elites are also structurally violent (table: category 3). That is to say, as analyses of the roles of imperial elites clearly indicate, societal leaders use their leadership positions and societal institutions (such as judicial processes, military personnel, and slavery[37]), along with their wealth, power, and alliances, to protect a vertical social structure that is of enormous benefit to themselves and of great harm to others.[38] Consistent with a basic principle of Roman justice, namely that punishment fits the societal (non)status of the person,[39] Jesus' crucifixion serves to protect elite interests against a provincial who challenges his assigned place in society, the elite's right to assign it, and the order of the society that the elite shapes.

But beyond this, the narrative of Jesus' ministry and crucifixion assumes and exposes a further dimension of their violence, namely the structural violence wrought by the vertical imperial social order shaped, imposed, and maintained by the elite. Agrarian imperial economies sustain their vertical social structure by (the threat of) military force[40] and by the use of taxation, loans, foreclosure, and debt to seize wealth for the benefit of the ruling elite. Such a structure has disastrous effects on the well-being of most of the population, depriving some 97 percent of the population of adequate resources, confining them with limited sociopolitical and economic opportunities, enslaving some, and denying access to processes of decision and change.[41] Any discernible[42] challenge to such a structure meets with harsh protective actions.

The structural violence that the elite imposes on the majority nonelite is assumed and evidenced by every chapter in the gospel. Three brief examples will suffice here. It is given graphic and metaphorical expression when Jesus describes the crowds he encounters in his Galilean preaching and healing tour as "harassed (ἐσκυλμένοι) and helpless (ἐρριμμένοι), like sheep without a shepherd" (9:36).[43] The first of the two participles, "harassed," denotes flaying or skinning, a graphic metaphor for violent and forcible plunder (BAGD, 758). The second, "helpless," literally means "thrown away" or "thrown or lying down" (BAGD, 736; cf. Matt 15:30 for sick people). Its Septuagint uses refer to people thrown away/down and destroyed by various kinds of violence including war and imperial violence (cf. Pharaoh's order in Exod 1:22). Jesus' words describe an oppressed, downtrodden, beaten-up, and crushed people. By what means? Jesus' subsequent description of these crowds as "sheep without a shepherd" (9:36b) points directly to the elite's imperial system. "Shepherds" is a common metaphor for rulers and kings,[44] and often in the biblical tradition for unfaithful leaders who take care only of their own interests. In Ezek 34, for example, these leaders rule with "force and harshness" (34:4, 17–19), deprive their charges of food and clothing, and provide no care for the sick, injured, and weak. The invitation to "come to me all who labor and are heavy laden" (11:28–30) embraces similar sociopolitical and economic structural violence,[45] as do the gospel's references to slavery (especially in parables, for example, 18:23–35; 21:33–41; 22:1–14; 25:14–30).[46]

The second example elaborates the first. The numerous sick and physically damaged folks who people the gospel in the healing and exorcism stories provide stark testimony to the violence that this hierarchical society enacts and the havoc it causes. The elite's conspicuous consumption of wealth and its quest for power, wealth, and status are sustained by goods and services exacted from the rest of the population through taxation and coercion (including slavery).[47] As numerous studies have observed, the resultant inadequate food supply, deficient nutrition, overwork, overcrowding, hard labor, indebtedness, poor sanitation, and physical and emotional stress suffered by most of the population caused enormous physical and psychological damage.[48] Jesus' response is not one of violence (from which he distances himself in 5:39–42 and 26:53–55), nor one of passive acquiescence. Rather, he articulates in his words ("the empire of the heavens," 4:17) and enacts in his deeds—healings (chapters 8–9; 11:2–6; cf. Isa 35:1–10), feedings (Matt 14:29–39; cf. Isa 25:6–10), exorcisms (Matt 12:22–32), community building (cf. 20:25–26)—an alternative vision of human society that embodies and anticipates God's rule and is marked by access to abundant resources for all.[49] His ministry reveals, opposes, and seeks to alleviate aspects of the impact of this structural violence. In crucifying him, the elite violently defeats this threat and protects its societal structure that does violence to most of the population. Jesus warns that disciples who continue to proclaim and enact the same challenging vision will encounter the same violent response (cf. 10:17–18; 23:34).

This structural violence is attested, thirdly, by the gospel's intertextuality or frequent citations of the Hebrew Scriptures, that is, Matthew's so-called fulfillment texts. Often the textual studies of the sources of these citations have missed an essential and larger point. In oral-derived narratives, citations perform what John Foley identifies as a metonymic function, evoking not just one verse but larger narratives.[50] These larger scriptural narratives evoked by Matthew's citations frequently concern imperial aggression by elites in the quest of power, territory, and human and nonhuman resources. Citations such as the double citing of Isa 7–9 in Matt 1:23 and 4:15–16 involve powers such as Egypt, Assyria, and Babylon, sometimes as agents of God's judgment and sometimes as thwarted by God and recipients of God's wrath. In turn, the citations comment on and interpret the gospel audience's present experience of the imperial world by means of past analogous situations involving imperial powers.[51]

The societal status quo ruled over by the elite, then, is marked by structural violence. The gospel presents this status quo as illegitimate because it is contrary to God's purposes.

Nonviolent Nonelites

Consistent with the gospel's attribution of violence to the elite is its construction of nonelites as generally not violent (table: category 5). The term "crowds" appears fifty times in the gospel to denote Galileans or Jerusalemites, depending on the context.[52] Mostly the crowds are presented as interested in, and at times receptive to, Jesus, in contrast with the elite's hostility (9:33–34; 12:23–24). And throughout the crowds are the victims of the elite's structural violence as Jesus points out in 9:36 (as considered in the previous section) and 11:28–30.[53]

It is probably in this latter context that the association of particular Jerusalem crowds with violence in two scenes, Jesus' arrest and his trial before Pilate, should be understood. In both scenes, Jerusalem crowds appear as instruments and extensions of the elite's violent structure. When Judas undertakes Jesus' arrest aided by "a large crowd with swords and clubs from the chief priests and elders," the crowds are clearly agents of the elite (26:47). They do not, however, actually act violently because Jesus, understanding the inevitability of his death (16:21 and others) and rejecting the option of violent divine intervention (26:53), does not resist arrest. That inevitability and his nonresistance emphasize how integral is violence, represented by the intimidating and armed large crowd, to the elite's way of being and accomplishing its will in the world.

In 27:15, 20, 25, a Jerusalem crowd calls for Jesus' death. The narrative mitigates its complicity in several ways. In 27:3a, the elite's commitment to put Jesus to death is unstoppable. In fact it is so inevitable that Judas hangs himself after he "saw that [Jesus] was condemned" (27:3a), eight verses *before* Jesus' "trial" with Pilate begins (27:11–26) and twenty-three verses *before* Pilate actually condemns him (27:26). And in 27:20 the elite manipulates this Jerusalem crowd to shout for the elite's goal.[54] By associating the crowd with the elite in both scenes, the narrative unmasks the elite's extensive control. In both scenes the crowds are local and particular, and do not represent all Jews.

The gospel's presentation of Barabbas, for whose release the manipulated crowd shouts (27:20–23), is vague in relation to violence. Matthew identifies him generically as a "notorious prisoner" rather than as a "bandit" or insurrectionist (cf. John 18:40), an explicitly political term denoting violence usually against elite personnel and property. I will discuss the significant exceptions to the construction of nonviolent nonelites (household violence in 10:21–22; table: categories 6–7) below.

Gender

I have suggested that ethnicity, long the most popular category for Matthean scholars, is not the determinative factor in the construction of violence in Matthew. I am obviously not suggesting that the gospel does not present any Jews as committing violence. The (Jerusalem) leaders (chief priests, scribes, Pharisees) figure prominently as agents of violence, as do synagogue authorities, and in the passion narratives, Jerusalem crowds contribute to the violence. I am suggesting, however, that the dominant (though not exclusive) association of violence with the ruling elite, both Jewish and Roman, indicates that social status plays a more important role than ethnicity.

But caution is necessary in constructing an elite versus nonelite binary. One could, for example, make the argument, based on the references discussed so far, that gender also plays a crucial role in constructing violence. Males commit violence, but females do not (though Herodias's complicity in John's death in 14:1–10 offers one exception). Male elites, then, are especially prone to commit violence.

But any claims that violence is uniquely associated with gender (male) or social status (elite) must be qualified by the references in chapter 10 (table: categories 6–7). The references to violence and hostility encountered in the context of mission and households described in chapter 10 are not specifically restricted to Jews even though the chapter's literary fiction emphasizes mission to Israel (10:5–6). And violence in chapter 10 is not restricted to elite figures. Certainly violence is presented as originating from elite males such as kings, governors, and synagogue officials in 10:17–18. But it also originates from persons in (village) household contexts, including children (10:21, 35), siblings (10:21), fathers (10:21), and daughters/daughters-in-law (10:35), but interestingly, not mothers. The inclusion of women indicates that violence is not an exclusively male characteristic. Chapter 10's domestic violence shows that while the gospel often constructs violence in terms of gender (male) and status (elite), ultimately binaries of male versus female and elite versus nonelite do not fully contain it. Rather, violence, significantly, seems to be evident in the gospel wherever God's empire is asserted.

Nonviolent Disciples

In contrast, the gospel constructs disciples as nonviolent (table: category 8). The relational violence of Judas's and Peter's betrayals of Jesus (and the betrayal by all of the disciples in 26:56) is clearly not a model to be imitated. While violent persecution of disciples is presented as normative and inevitable (10:17–18; 13:21; 23:34), disciples are forbidden to inflict violence on others.[55] As Walter Wink has shown, they cannot use violent means to resist evildoers (5:39), but they are to employ nonviolent ways of resistance,[56] along with love and prayer (5:44). In one instance, "one who was with Jesus" responds violently in cutting off the ear of the high priest's slave (26:51). But the scene rejects this violent behavior. While his being "with Jesus" suggests he was a disciple,[57] his sword signals his ignorance of both Jesus' prohibition of violence (5:39) and the inevitability of Jesus' death (16:21). Further, Jesus' immediate rebuke of his action emphasizes that violence is not an option for disciples. Interestingly, the gospel does not indicate whether the construction of the disciples as nonviolent reflects and reinforces the gospel audience's "normal" nonviolent social intercourse, or aims to counter and correct violent social actions by and among community members.

Theological Violence: Satan, God, and Jesus

Thus far, I have argued that the gospel often constructs male elites (Gentile and Jewish) and their social-political-religious status quo as inherently violent. But violence is not restricted to them as the household references to violence against disciples in chapter 10 make clear. Hence the category of social status, like that of ethnicity and gender, usefully identifies a crucial element of the gospel's construction of violence, but ultimately it is not fully adequate for the task.

I would argue that violence for Matthew is ultimately an ideological, or more specifically, a theological construct. References to Satan (table: category 9) and God (table: category 10) suggest that violence is both cosmic and theological. The presentation of the devil is instructive. The devil's empire (13:38–39) opposes God's purposes in the world (13:38–39), whether manifested by John (11:12), Jesus (4:1–11), or disciples (13:19). The devil is the power behind the thrones, claiming authority over "all the empires (βασιλείας, 4:8) of the world," notably Rome, and using empires as its agents so that the elite resembles and embodies the devil's tempting and evil agenda (cf. 4:1, 3 with 16:1 and 19:3; cf. 6:13 and 13:38 with 9:4 and 16:4). The violent world under the elite's control is the devil's work.

That is, the world that does not follow Jesus is presented, stereotypically, as an illegitimate structure that resists God's purposes to "bless all the nations of the earth" (Matt 1:1, "son of Abraham," evoking Abraham in Gen 12:1–3). Those who do not follow Jesus, especially but not exclusively male elites, employ violence to structure a status quo that counters God's purposes. Violence is not just a means of coercion in the service of greed or power or furthering elite interests, though it is indeed that. The gospel discloses/constructs it to be an activity of the devil, an activity that rejects the gospel of God's empire when and as it affects the present way of life (so 11:12; 10:22; 24:9; table: category 11). The particular, though not exclusive, penchant for violence among male elites suggests that power groups in a patriarchal and vertical society find the announcement of God's purposes, whether proclaimed by prophets, by Jesus, or by disciples, to be especially disturbing or threatening to the status quo and their self-interest. Household members are also threatened. Violence is constructed as the way of the world.[58] Significantly, it is the gospel that provides the perspective that unmasks the true cosmic and theological nature of the social-political-religious violence.

What, then, are we to make of God's eschatological violence, Jesus' destructive *parousia* and resultant eschatological battle (24:27–31), and his pervasive violent rhetoric against his opponents? As Barbara Reid has observed, the violent scenarios of eschatological judgment are clearly at odds with the emphasis on the disciples' nonviolent participation in the present.[59] Violence is the activity of God, not disciples, and is reserved for the future, not the present. Those who refuse God's life-giving way will then reap the violent eschatological consequences of their commitment to violence. As Jesus observes, to take the sword is to perish by the sword (26:52).

Jesus' violent rhetoric, references to violence, and acts of violence should be read in this context. His claim in 10:34 not to bring peace but a sword is usually understood metaphorically to refer to the conflict and division that Jesus' ministry causes. But as Davies and Allison observe, the sword is also associated with eschatological judgment (for example, Isa 66:16).[60] That judgment is under way in Jesus' ministry manifested in people's responses, and will be completed at Jesus' return. Jesus' physically violent disruption of the temple in 21:12-17 foreshadows the destruction and punishment of the elite's center of power (Jerusalem and the temple) at Rome's hands in 70 C.E. (22:7), and anticipates the final violent judgment effected in the cosmic war that marks Jesus' return (24:27-31).[61] So too do his rhetorically violent assertion that the Jerusalem elite have no place in God's purposes (15:13), his description of them as "evil" like Satan (cf. 12:34; 16:1-4 and 6:13; also tempters in 16:1 and 4:1-3), and his scathing series of condemnatory woes against them (chapter 23). His exorcisms, his "throwing out" of demons (8:16; 9:33, 38 and more) and of the temple officials (21:12), evidence the struggle with Satan and victory of God's empire (12:24-28).

Functions

How do the depictions of God's eschatological violence function? I suggest that, like the construction of the resisting world as violent and of disciples as nonviolent, they contribute to the construction of boundaries for Matthew's community and to the identity of disciples as the minority suffering righteous who live liminally awaiting God's vindication.[62]

The gospel employs the extensive biblical tradition of the righteous sufferer, embracing variously the suffering poor (Matt 5:5; Ps 37), the lamenting righteous (cf. Jesus the nonviolent righteous sufferer, Matt 26-27),[63] those oppressed by imperial powers (the suffering servant, Isa 42; 52-53, cited in Matt 8:17; 12:18-21; evoked by 26:62-63; 27:12-14), and the rejected prophet (5:10-12; 23:34). Such people are opposed by the powerful (Jewish and Gentile) elite that readily employs violence (physical, structural, rhetorical) to maintain its societal position and power. The poor, the prophet, the oppressed have little option but to absorb the elite's societal violence, to exercise selective and self-protective nonviolent resistance,[64] and to look to God for vindication.

This identity of disciples as righteous sufferers also involves practices. The eschatological depictions legitimate the nonviolent practice of disciples in the present. Disciples can "afford" this nonviolent stance because the apocalyptic worldview affirms the coming triumph of God and of believers. Disciples can endure nonviolently in the meantime because, in the end, God will punish the opponents, just as God has already punished the Jerusalem elite, ironically at Rome's hands, in the war that ended in 70 C.E. (22:7).

Vivienne Jabri argues that the construction of exclusionary identities centered on membership in bounded communities and constituted by discursive and institutional dividing lines is "a central feature in the emergence of violence."[65] Matthew's gospel constructs violence—its predictable presence among those who do not follow Jesus, its absence from disciples, its eschatological consequences—as a hallmark of a division that is domestic, societal, and cosmic. Whether such a construction makes sense because of actual violence against and/or by disciples, or because of imagined or feared or rumored violence, or because of all of the above, is difficult to know. Some recent studies of millennialist groups, however, may offer a clue.

Jabri's emphasis on exclusionary identities and entexted dividing lines receives support from Catherine Wessinger's collection of studies, *Millennialism, Persecution, and Violence.*[66] Wessinger identifies the sort of apocalyptic thinking evident in Matthew as "catastrophic millennialism." In contrast to "progressive millennialism" in which humans progressively establish the kingdom, catastrophic millennialism (which she equates with biblical apocalyptic thinking) sees God or another superhuman agent intervening to accomplish the transition to the millennial kingdom, thereby bringing the present evil world to an end. She argues that groups can move between these forms of millennialism, but the form of millennialism adopted often correlates with their levels of societal (dis)comfort or (non)accommodation. When "disaster, opposition, or persecution is encountered, catastrophic themes will receive greater prominence." Also typical of catastrophic millennialism is a "radical dualistic view" that "divides people into good vs. evil, us vs. them, and the human vs. the inhuman, demonic, and less than human." In dehumanizing opponents, as does Matthew's text, such dualism, she argues, stimulates violence, whether from a millennialist group that arms itself to combat diabolical forces, or from the powerful members of the status quo who attack the millennialist group as a threat to public order and their vested interests.

Crucial to these divisions and dualisms is the gospel's apocalyptic mindset or worldview of a cosmic war in which God and believers triumph (24:27–31). In his study of contemporary religious violence, *Terror in the Mind of God,* Mark Juergensmeyer argues that such "grand scenarios," as he calls them, are crucial in situations of violent conflict over matters that participants deem to be of ultimate significance.[67] The worldview involves a "dichotomous opposition on an absolute scale," an "all-or-nothing struggle" against an enemy that is to be destroyed, an utter "certitude" about one's own convictions that allows no compromise, negotiation (cf. 22:46), or coexistence. Grand scenarios are rooted in convictions that the world under its present ruling powers has gone horribly astray, an analysis evident to only a few, but an analysis that makes sense of the present distress and locates believers in the cosmic battle against evil in which they will finally be victorious. Grand scenarios originate "in hopeless moments, when mythical strength provides the only resources at hand." They concern visions of how society is to be ordered, who does the ordering, who controls the resources, who benefits at whose expense, and who or what sanctions the present and the (new) future. Grand scenarios are, then, ultimately about power, functioning for the desperate minority group to reveal and contest current structures and to empower faithful perseverance and appropriate opposition until the new world dawns.

In Jabri's terms, Matthew's discourse of God's eschatological violence locates the righteous followers of Matthew's Jesus socially in a bounded, harassed, and nonviolent community, and cosmically and theologically in God's purposes in which they, the suffering righteous, will be vindicated. It simultaneously excludes nonfollowers of Jesus and marks them, the oppressive (male) elite in particular, but not exclusively, as reaping the violent consequences of their violent social structure and inevitable violent rejection of God's purposes (26:52). That is, Matthew's "grand scenario" vindicates a vision of the world, articulated and enacted by Jesus' deeds and words, as the ultimate expression of God's will. Simultaneously, it delegitimizes, contests, and denies such a claim to the present world as ordered by the social-political-religious leaders of Rome and Jerusalem. In this way, Matthew answers the question that is, according to Ernst Käsemann, central for apocalyptic grand scenarios: "To whom does the sovereignty of the world belong?"[68]

Matthew's Gospel thus constructs violence theologically. It regards it as central to the sinful human societal situation from which Jesus is to save people (1:21); as deeply enmeshed in and expressed by the current elite-dominated, imperial, societal structure; as inevitable to the conflict over the competing societal visions that come into sharp collision through Jesus' life and death; and as crucial to the divine completion of that salvation in Jesus' return and resultant judgment. In resisting and redeeming the violence of the imperial status quo, the gospel also affirms that some violence, namely the violence of God, the supreme ruler who is "Lord of heaven and earth (11:25), and of God's agent Jesus, is legitimate and necessary.

Given Jesus' rhetorically violent condemnation of the status quo, his physically violent anticipation of judgment in his temple actions, and the violent visions of God's eschatological triumph accomplished through Jesus' *parousia* and eschatological battle, Matthew's gospel finally, but ironically, capitulates to and imitates the imperial violence from which it seeks to save.

Notes

1. Warren Carter, "Pilate and Jesus: Roman Justice All Washed Up," in *Matthew and Empire: Initial Explorations* (Harrisburg, Pa.: Trinity Press International, 2001), 145–68; idem, *Pontius Pilate: Portraits of a Roman Governor* (Interfaces; Collegeville, Minn.: Liturgical Press, 2003), 75–99; contra, for example, Helen Bond, *Pontius Pilate in History and Interpretation* (SNTSMS 100; Cambridge: Cambridge University Press, 1998), 120–37.

2. Shelly Matthews, "Ethical Issues in Reconstructing Intra-Jewish Violence in Antiquity: The Gospel of Matthew as a Test Case," in *Walk in the Ways of Wisdom: Essays in Honor of Elizabeth Schüssler Fiorenza* (ed. Shelly Matthews, Cynthia Kittredge, and Melanie Johnson-DeBaufre; Harrisburg, Pa.: Trinity Press International, 2003), 334–50. Matthews provides examples of this approach from the work of James Sanders, David Sim, Graham Stanton, Ulrich Luz, and Douglas Hare.

3. David Frankfurter ("Response," paper presented at the annual meeting of the SBL, Toronto, 2002) raises the possibility that Matthew elaborates "the Q-document, which is also inordinately preoccupied with persecution" and wonders if "an ideology of persecution and vengeance" has been "inherited and internalized." One could add Mark as another possibility, though adding either tradition simply shifts the question of origin and function: What is happening that allows such self-definition and boundary-drawing to be so meaningful? Matthew is convinced that disciples imitate Jesus in being recipients of violence (10:24–25), sustaining my argument here that elite violence generated by defending societal interests is a primary Matthean concern.

4. Matthews ("Ethical Issues," 348–50) highlights the only extant first-century text not written by a follower of Jesus that narrates an act of violence against Jewish followers of Jesus by Jews who are not followers, namely Josephus's account of the high priest Ananus's stoning of James the brother of Jesus for transgressing the law. Josephus states that the execution caused other Jews in Jerusalem, including the "fair-minded" and "strict observers of the law," to be offended or grieved, and Ananus to be removed from the priesthood (*Ant.* 20.200–203). Matthews asks what difference it would make to historical reconstructions of intra-Jewish violence involving followers of Jesus if this text became the starting point.

5. Catherine Wessinger, ed., *Millennialism, Persecution, and Violence: Historical Cases* (Syracuse, N.Y.: Syracuse University Press, 2000), 43–118. The case studies in the volume that fall under this classification include Mormons, the Lakota massacred at Wounded Knee, David Koresh's Branch Davidians, and Rastafarians in the Caribbean island of Dominica.

6. For discussion of conflict/violence as constructed discourse, see Vivienne Jabri, "The Construction of Identity and the Discourse of Violence," in *Discourses on Violence: Conflict Analysis Reconsidered* (Manchester: Manchester University Press, 1996), 119–44.

7. One recent discussion (Matthews, "Ethical Issues," 340–41) highlights the role of these five texts in numerous discussions. Neither I nor Matthews is claiming a comprehensive summary of all Matthean scholarship.

8. Warren Carter, *Matthew and the Margins* (Maryknoll, N.Y.: Orbis, 2000; Sheffield: Sheffield Academic Press, 2000), 130–37; Mark Powell, "Matthew's Beatitudes: Reversals and Rewards of the Kingdom," *CBQ* 58 (1996): 460–79.

9. On metonymic intertextuality, see John Miles Foley, *Immanent Art: From Structure to Meaning in Traditional Oral Epic* (Bloomington: Indiana University Press, 1991).

10. For discussion of historically plausible scenarios envisioned by the text, see Dorothy Jean Weaver, *Matthew's Missionary Discourse: A Literary Critical Analysis* (JSNTSup 38; Sheffield Academic Press, 1990), 93–95; Ulrich Luz, *Matthew 8–20* (Hermeneia; Minneapolis: Fortress Press, 2001), 87–93; Douglas Hare, *The Theme of Jewish Persecution of Christians in the Gospel According to St. Matthew* (Cambridge: Cambridge University Press, 1967), 43–46. Councils are probably local councils. Paul attests flogging by synagogue authorities in 2 Cor 11:25. Flogging, repeated in 23:34 for followers and in 20:19 for Jesus, is prescribed as a punishment in Deut 25:1–3 for the party judged to be wrong in a dispute. The text does not stipulate for what wrong Jesus' followers are to be flogged. William Davies and Dale Allison (*The Gospel According to Matthew* [ICC; Edinburgh: T&T Clark, 1991], 2:183) speculate that the wrong may comprise evil speaking against leaders and/or making claims about Jesus considered to be blasphemous. Hare (*Theme,* 46) concludes there is no evidence for flogging as a penalty for profession of Christ.

How "violent" is the treatment by Gentiles? The verb ἀχθήσεσθε is used in Matthew 10:18 with a sense of both custody and trial. Peter Garnsey (*Social Status and Legal Privilege in the Roman Empire* [Oxford: Clarendon, 1970]) demonstrates that Roman justice was not disinterested, but served to reinforce social verticality with its variable treatments of defendants in which social status played a most significant role. In this sense Roman justice is an instrument of the elite's control that does violence to the rest of society (the "wide" definition of violence below).

11. The text does not specify how this might be accomplished.

12. They employ attributive participles "equivalent to a relative clause" (BDF, no. 412) and the relative pronoun with both the indicative and subjunctive.

13. For discussion, Carter, *Matthew and the Margins*, 426–31.

14. Matthean scholarship has overlooked Anthony J. Saldarini, *Pharisees, Scribes, and Sadducees in Palestinian Society* (Wilmington, Del.: Michael Glazier, 1988); Carter, *Matthew and the Margins*, passim. See note 29.

15. Witness a further related strand that Jerusalem remains God's city (5:35), a holy city (4:5; 27:53) called to serve God.

16. 1 Sam 30:6; 1 Kgs 19:10; 2 Chr 36:11–16; Neh 9:26; Jer 2:30; *4 Bar.* 9:21–32; *Liv. Pro.* 2:1. For nonviolent rejection, Isa 30:10; Amos 2:11–12.

17. For elite figures (kings, queens, priests, officials, etc.) killing prophets: 1 Kgs 18:4, 13; 2 Chr 24:20–21; 25:16 (threatened); 36:11–16 (rejecting, along with "the people"); Jer 26:20–23; *Liv. Pro.* 3:2; 23:1; *Mart. Ascen. Isa.* 2:12–16. For violent, nonfatal actions against prophets by elites: 1 Kgs 22:24; Jer 20:1–2; 37:15; 38:4–6; Josephus, *Ant.* 4:22 and *J.W.* 6.302. For nonviolent elite resistance: Amos 7:10–13. For elite violence against John: Matt 14:12; and against Jesus: 16:21 and others. For further discussion, see the contribution in this volume of Melanie Johnson-DeBaufre, "The Blood Required of This Generation: Interpreting Communal Blame in a Colonial Context."

18. Matt 2:6, 20, 21; 8:10; 9:33; 10:6, 23; 15:24, 31; 19:28; 27:9, 42.

19. To illustrate the problem, I have not included on the chart, for example, the questioning of Jesus' honor and public reputation in 13:53–58 (arguably a doing of violence to his honor), the eating of fish in 14:13–21 (doing violence in causing the death of living creatures), the violent wind and sea in 14:22–33, or the earthquakes that accompany Jesus' death (27:51), resurrection (28:3), and anticipate his return (24:7). I have included some of the parables twice, under different sections (18:23–35; 22:1–14).

20. The bibliography is immense. In addition to the material listed below, I have found the following work on religious violence interesting: R. Scott Appleby, *The Ambivalence of the Sacred: Religion, Violence, and Reconciliation* (Lanham, Md.: Rowman & Littlefield, 2000); Marc Ellis, *Unholy Alliance: Religion and Atrocity in Our Time* (Minneapolis: Fortress Press, 1997); Leo Lefebure, *Revelation, the Religions, and Violence* (Maryknoll, N.Y.: Orbis, 2000); Hent de Vries, *Religion and Violence: Philosophical Perspectives from Kant to Derrida* (Baltimore: Johns Hopkins University Press, 2002); Stephen Stein, "The Web of Religion and Violence," *RelSRev* 28 (April 2002): 103–8.

21. C. A. J. Coady, "The Idea of Violence," in *Violence and Its Alternatives: An Interdisciplinary Reader* (ed. Manfred Steger and Nancy Lind; New York: St. Martin's Press, 1999), 23–38, esp. 24. Coady's preference is for the first, or restricted, definition.

22. Coady ("Idea of Violence," 29) quotes Harris's definition: "An act of violence occurs when injury or suffering is inflicted upon a person or persons by an agent who

knows (or ought reasonably to have known) that his actions would result in the harm in question."

23. Coady ("Idea of Violence," 24) quotes, for example, the definition of Newton Garver: "The institutional form of quiet violence operates when people are deprived of choices in a systematic way by the very manner in which transactions normally take place"; and of Johan Galtung (25), "Violence is present when human beings are being influenced so that their actual somatic and mental realizations are below their potential realizations." For Galtung's approach, see his essay "Cultural Violence," in *Violence and Its Alternatives: An Interdisciplinary Reader* (ed. Manfred Steger and Nancy Lind; New York: St. Martin's Press, 1999), 39–53.

24. Robert Wolff, "On Violence," in *Violence and Its Alternatives: An Interdisciplinary Reader* (ed. Manfred Steger and Nancy Lind; New York: St. Martin's Press, 1999), 12–22. Wolff defines violence as "the illegitimate or unauthorized use of force to effect decisions against the will or desire of others" (33).

25. Galtung, "Cultural Violence," 39.

26. Sharon Ringe, *Jesus, Liberation, and the Biblical Jubilee: Images for Ethics and Christology* (OBT 19; Philadelphia: Fortress Press, 1985), passim.

27. Carter, *Matthew and the Margins,* 130–37.

28. Hare (*Theme,* 80–96, 105–6) observes in this section increased polemic against scribes and Pharisees, but sees it not only as literary polemic but also as reflective of some historical circumstances concerning former Christian missionary activity.

29. See Hare (*Theme,* 114–21) against Christian prophets in mission to Israel; Davies and Allison (*Matthew,* 1.462–63) wonder if specific situations (ban from the synagogue) or general ones (religious jokes? accusations in court?) are in view; Carter (*Matthew and the Margins,* 137) suggests slander and defaming.

30. On scribes as elite members of imperial societies, see Saldarini, *Pharisees, Scribes, and Sadducees.* I am not questing for the historical Pharisees. Rather I am taking note of the alliance of leadership people variously identified as scribes, Pharisees, Sadducees, and priests that the gospel establishes. For example, scribes are introduced with chief priests as Herod's allies in 2:4; scribes and Pharisees are associated in 5:20; Pharisees are allied with the chief priests in 27:62.

31. For example, Gerhard Lenski, *Power and Privilege: A Theory of Social Stratification* (New York: McGraw-Hill, 1966), 189–296.

32. The judicial functions of the synagogue were in the hands of leaders, often identified as ἄρχοντες or ἀρχιπροστάται, though roles and titles were by no means fixed and ἀρχισυνάγωγοι may also have exercised this function. So Donald Binder, *Into The Temple Courts: The Place of the Synagogue in the Second Temple Period* (SBLDS 169; Atlanta: SBL, 1999), 343–55. Binder's discussion of the leadership terms' widespread uses and the functions that they denote indicates that leadership positions required wealth, education, political knowledge and leadership, and elite status. See also T. Rajak and D. Noy, "Archisynagogoi: Office, Title, and Social Status in the Greco-Jewish Synagogue," *JRS* 83 (1993): 75–93. For the flogging of the prophet Jesus son of Ananias by "some of the leading citizens," see Josephus, *J. W.* 6.302.

33. See Carter, *Matthew and Empire*, 9–53.

34. As I erroneously do in my earlier work, *Matthew: Storyteller, Interpreter, Evangelist* (Peabody, Mass.: Hendrickson, 1996). See the expanded and revised edition of 2004.

35. Lenski, *Power and Privilege*, 189–296.

36. Carter, *Matthew and the Margins*, 426–37.

37. The literature on slavery is vast. See Orlando Patterson, *Slavery and Social Death: A Comparative Study* (Cambridge, Mass.: Harvard University Press, 1982); Keith Hopkins, *Slavery and Society in Rome* (Cambridge: Cambridge University Press, 1994); Richard A. Horsley, "The Slave Systems of Classical Antiquity and Their Reluctant Recognition by Modern Scholars," *Semeia* 83/84 (1998): 19–66. The irony is not to be missed that frequently the gospel reinscribes this structure while employing it as a metaphor for service to God. See also Warren Carter, *Households and Discipleship: A Study of Matthew 19–20* (JSNTSup 103; Sheffield: JSOT Press, 1994), 172–92; idem, "Imperial Paradigms in the Parables of Matthew 18:21–35 and 22:1–14," *Interpretation* 56 (2002): 260–72. Jennifer A. Glancy (*Slavery in Early Christianity* [New York: Oxford University Press, 2002], 112–22) emphasizes the physically violent treatment of slaves in Matthew.

38. For social analyses of imperial or agrarian societies, see Lenski, *Power and Privilege*, 189–296; John Kautsky, *The Politics of Aristocratic Empires* (Chapel Hill: University of North Carolina Press, 1982); Michael Mann, "Roman Territorial Empire," in A History of Power From the Beginning to A.D. 1760 (vol. 1 of The Sources of Social Power; Cambridge: Cambridge University Press, 1986), 250–300. For discussion of particular Matthean texts, see Carter, *Matthew and the Margins*; also Carter, *Matthew and Empire*, 9–53.

39. Garnsey, *Social Status and Legal Privilege*.

40. Susan Mattern, *Rome and the Enemy: Imperial Strategy in the Principate* (Berkeley: University of California Press, 1999).

41. Lenski, *Power and Privilege*, 189–296; Kautsky, *Politics*; Mann, "Roman Territorial Empire," 250–300; Carter, *Matthew and the Margins*; also idem, *Matthew and Empire*, 9–53.

42. I include the adjective "discernible" in recognition of Scott's argument that lower-ranked societal members like peasants constantly find "hidden" ways to contest the power of their rulers. James Scott, *Weapons of the Weak: Everyday Forms of Peasant Resistance* (New Haven, Conn.: Yale University Press, 1985).

43. For discussion and references, see Carter, *Matthew and the Margins*, 230–31.

44. Suetonius (*Tib.* 32) has the emperor Tiberius reject a governor's plan to impose further harsh taxes on his province by saying that "it was the part of a good shepherd to shear his flock, not skin it."

45. For discussion, Carter, *Matthew and Empire*, 108–29.

46. For discussion, see note 37, and the relevant sections in Carter, *Matthew and the Margins*, and Glancy, *Slavery*, 112–22.

47. Tacitus (*Ann.* 13.50) presents a scene in which Nero's advisers persuade Nero not to abolish "all indirect taxation" because "the dissolution of the empire was certain

if the revenues on which the state subsisted were to be curtailed." Carter, *Matthew and Empire*, 9–50.

48. John Pairman Brown, "Techniques of Imperial Control: The Background of the Gospel Event," in *The Bible and Liberation: Political and Social Hermeneutics* (ed. Norman Gottwald; Maryknoll, N.Y.: Orbis, 1983), 357–77; Paul Hollenbach, "Jesus, Demoniacs, and Public Authorities," *JAAR* 49 (1981): 567–88; Gerd Theissen, *The Miracle Stories in Early Christian Tradition* (Philadelphia: Fortress Press, 1982), 231–64; Rodney Stark, "Antioch as the Social Situation for Matthew's Gospel," in *Social History of the Matthean Community* (ed. David Balch; Minneapolis: Fortress Press, 1991), 189–210; Peter Garnsey, *Food and Society in Classical Antiquity* (Cambridge: Cambridge University Press, 1999); Carter, *Matthew and the Margins*, 17–29, 36–43, 123–27, 196–98.

49. Walter Wink, "Beyond Just War and Pacifism: Jesus' Nonviolent Way," *RevExp* 89 (1992): 197–214; idem, "Neither Passivity nor Violence: Jesus' Third Way (Matt 5:38–42 par.)," in *The Love of Enemy and Nonretaliation in the New Testament* (ed. Willard Swartley; Louisville, Ky.: Westminster John Knox, 1992), 102–25; Carter, *Matthew and the Margins*; and idem, *Matthew and Empire*.

50. Foley, *Immanent Art*.

51. Warren Carter, "Evoking Isaiah: Why Summon Isaiah in Matthew 1:23 and 4:15–16?" in *Matthew and Empire*, 93–107; also in *JBL* 119 (2000): 503–20.

52. Warren Carter, "The Crowds in Matthew's Gospel," *CBQ* 55 (1993): 54–67.

53. See Carter, *Matthew and Empire*, 108–29.

54. Ibid., 145–68.

55. Cf. the thesis of Judith Perkins, *The Suffering Self: Pain and Narrative Representation in the Early Christian Era* (London: Routledge, 1995), which argues from post-first-century texts that a new Christian subjectivity centered on suffering emerges. Perkins explicitly excludes New Testament and first-century texts from her inquiry (13).

56. Wink, "Beyond Just War"; "Neither Passivity nor Violence."

57. Hubert Frankemölle, *Jahwebund und Kirche Christi* (NTAbh 10; Münster: Aschendorff, 1974), chapter 1.

58. Luz (*Matthew 8–20*, 88) comes close to this conclusion in commenting on 10:17–18, "All unbelievers are dangerous."

59. Barbara Reid, "Violent Endings in Matthew's Parables and an End to Violence" (paper presented at the annual meeting of the SBL, Denver, Colorado, 2001).

60. Davies and Allison, *Matthew*, 2.218–19.

61. Warren Carter, "Intertextual Eagles and Matthean Eschatology as Lights out Time for Imperial Rome (Matt 24:27–31)," *JBL* 122 (2003): 467–87.

62. For Matthean discipleship as liminal existence, see Carter, *Households and Discipleship*.

63. Carter, *Matthew and the Margins*, 498.

64. For the role of masked or shrouded resistance among peasant and oppressed groups, see Scott, *Weapons*.

65. Jabri, "Construction of Identity," 120.

66. In what follows, I am especially drawing on Wessinger, *Millennialism*, 3–16.

67. Mark Juergensmeyer, *Terror in the Mind of God: The Global Rise of Religious Violence* (Berkeley: University of California Press, 2000), esp. 145–63. Against René Girard (*Violence and the Sacred* [Baltimore: Johns Hopkins University Press, 1977]), Juergensmeyer emphasizes the role not of sacrifice but of cosmic war in religious violence. But he does not want to argue that grand scenarios *inevitably* lead to violence. He recognizes that rituals and symbols that accompany grand scenarios can, though not always, prevent violent acts by channeling the "urges to conquer and control."

68. Ernst Käsemann, "On the Subject of Primitive Christian Apocalyptic," in *New Testament Questions of Today* (Philadelphia: Fortress Press, 1969), 108–37, esp. 135.

6

Love, Hate, and Violence in the Gospel of John*

ADELE REINHARTZ

During the night leading up to his betrayal, arrest, trial, and crucifixion, according to the Fourth Gospel, Jesus spoke at length with his disciples (John 13–16). In the course of these farewell speeches, he gave them a "new commandment": "that you love one another. Just as I have loved you, you also should love one another. By this everyone will know that you are my disciples, if you have love for one another" (13:34–35). Later on that night, Jesus reiterates this love command: "As the Father has loved me, so I have loved you; abide in my love. If you keep my commandments, you will abide in my love, just as I have kept my Father's commandments and abide in his love. I have said these things to you so that my joy may be in you, and that your joy may be complete. This is my commandment, that you love one another as I have loved you" (15:9–12).

It is not surprising, then, that the Gospel of John, in some circles at least, is known as the Gospel of Love.[1] But there is an irony here as well. Jesus' new commandment notwithstanding, the Gospel of Love has also been an instrument of hate, not once, not occasionally, but frequently and pervasively in the history of Jewish-Christian relations. Of course, the Gospel of John is not single-handedly responsible for Western anti-Semitism. Nevertheless, it has supplied one of the most persistent anti-Semitic images of all time: the Jew as the devil. From medieval sketches,[2] through Shakespeare,[3] to white Aryan Internet websites,[4] verbal and visual images

* This essay is a slightly revised version of an article that appears in Michael Labahn, Klaus Scholtissek, and Angelika Strothmann, eds., *Israel und seine Heilstraditionen im Johannesevangelium: Festgabe für Johannes Beutler SJ zum 70. Geburtstag* (Schöningh: Ferdinand, GmbH, Verlag, 2003), 416–27.

of the Jew as devil illustrate the legacy of John 8:44, in which Jesus declares to his Jewish opponents: "You are from your father the devil and you choose to do your father's desires. He was a murderer from the beginning and does not stand in the truth because there is no truth in him. When he lies, he speaks according to his own nature, for he is a liar and the father of lies." Throughout John's Gospel, the powerful associations of the Jews with darkness, death, and destruction (3:19, 8:24, 2:19) deliver a message of hate that does not sit well with the theme of love that Jesus announces in his farewell discourses.

Let me be clear. I am not suggesting that John 8:44 conveys the actual words of the historical Jesus. Neither would I argue that the Gospel's author or authors intended to sow the sort of hatred we now call anti-Semitism, or that they could have predicted the destructive use to which the Fourth Gospel has been put over time. Nevertheless, the contradiction between the commandment to love and the incitement to hate not only belongs to later interpretations of the Gospel but is also inherent in the text itself.

In this paper, I will attempt to place the vocabularies of love and hate in their literary contexts in the Fourth Gospel. This will entail looking carefully at the Gospel story itself and at the language in which it is told. Second, I will propose one way to account for the seeming contradiction between the language of love and the language of hate in the context of the history and experience of the community within which and for which the Gospel was written.

Love and hate are abstract nouns denoting emotions. In keeping with its intense christocentric nature, that is, its unremitting focus on Jesus in his identity as the Christ and Son of God, the Gospel of John defines love and hate entirely with respect to a person's stance toward Jesus. The love between Jesus and his followers flows entirely and solely from their faith in Jesus as the Messiah and Son of God; Jesus' accusation that the Jews are children of the devil is grounded in their refusal to believe in him.

Faith and disbelief, in turn, are closely linked to specific behaviors. Jesus' followers express their faith and love precisely in the fact that they follow him: they follow him physically as he travels around Judea, Samaria, and the Galilee, and they follow in his footsteps by preaching his word and, if need be, suffering for his sake. The Jews express their disbelief by their violent behavior. Indeed, the Jews' violence toward Jesus is the force that drives the plot of the Gospel, from their first encounter to the moment of his crucifixion. To the question of who did what to whom, the

Gospel answers: The Jews killed Jesus. In grammatical terms, the subject, that is, the actors, are the Jews, the verbs denote violent acts, and the object, or victim of those acts, is Jesus. A closer examination will show that this simple grammatical structure pervades the Gospel narrative.

The Jews' violent intentions toward Jesus first emerge in chapter 5. One Sabbath day, Jesus heals a lame man by the pool of Bethesda. When the Jewish authorities challenge Jesus for doing this, he answers, "My Father is still working, and I also am working" (5:17). Then the narrator explains: "For this reason the Jews were seeking all the more to kill him, because he was not only breaking the sabbath, but was also calling God his own Father, thereby making himself equal to God" (5:18). In grammatical terms, the subject of the narrator's explanatory sentence is "the Jews." The verb is "sought to kill," and the object of this verb is Jesus. Later, Jesus fears death at the hands of the Jews. The narrator tells us that after he fed the multitudes, Jesus "went about in Galilee. He did not wish to go about in Judea because the Jews were looking for an opportunity to kill him" (7:1). The subject of the subordinate clause ("because the Jews . . .") is the Jews; the verbal clause is "looking for an opportunity to kill," and the object is "him," meaning Jesus. Not only the narrator but Jesus himself accuses the Jews of attempting to kill him. In 7:19, Jesus confronts the Jews: "Did not Moses give you the law? Yet none of you keeps the law. Why are you looking for an opportunity to kill me?" Similarly, in 8:37, he declares to them: "I know that you are descendants of Abraham; yet you look for an opportunity to kill me, because there is no place in you for my word." These words are reinforced by the behavior of the Jews themselves. According to the narrator in 8:59, "the Jews picked up stones to throw at him," an action they repeat in 10:31. Finally, the Jewish leaders accuse Jesus to Pontius Pilate, and call for his crucifixion, shouting "Crucify him!" when it appears that Pilate is inclined to set Jesus free (19:6, 15).

The Gospel suggests various motivations for the Jews' violent intentions and acts against Jesus. Jesus himself believes that the Jews are reacting to his impressive and often transgressive deeds. As Jesus says in 10:32, "I have shown you many good works from the Father. For which of these are you going to stone me?" But the Jews counter: "It is not for a good work that we are going to stone you, but for blasphemy, because you, though only a human being, are making yourself God."

The charge of blasphemy also underlies the Jews' attempts to use legal channels in their campaign against Jesus. The Jews repeatedly try to arrest him (7:44, 10:39). Caiaphas, the high priest, suggests yet another motivation—not works, not blasphemy, but political expedience. As he says to other Jewish leaders, "You know nothing at all! You do not understand that it is better for you to have one man die for the people than to have the whole nation destroyed." "So from that day on," continues the narrator, "they planned to put him to death" (11:49–50, 53). The trial scenes highlight the legal backdrop as the Jewish leaders attempt to persuade Pilate that "We have a law, and according to that law he ought to die because he has claimed to be the Son of God" (19:7). The simple grammatical structure—the Jews stone Jesus, the Jews arrest Jesus, the Jews seek to kill Jesus, or to have him put to death—remains constant, rendering the later anti-Jewish and anti-Semitic charge of deicide—that is, the charge that the Jews killed Jesus—comprehensible if no less reprehensible.

To be sure, other characters in the Fourth Gospel also engage in violence. After Jesus' death sentence, Pilate's soldiers crown Jesus with thorns, mock him, and strike him (19:2–3). Despite the narrator's best efforts to cast blame solely on the Jewish leaders (cf. 19:15–16), Pilate bears some responsibility for Jesus' violent death as the one who formally hands Jesus over for crucifixion (19:16). Neither does Jesus refrain entirely from violence. When Jesus "cleanses" the temple, he drives out the merchants and money-changers with a whip of cords, and he overturns the tables (2:13–16). Immediately after Jesus' arrest, Simon Peter draws his sword and strikes the high priest's slave, cutting off his right ear (18:10).

But their literary contexts downplay these violent acts. The Roman soldiers are merely sporting with a man condemned to die through no doing of their own. Jesus' outburst in the temple is cast as Jesus' legitimate attempt to oust unwelcome elements that are defiling his Father's house (2:16). Simon Peter is admonished by Jesus for his impulsive defense of Jesus: "Put your sword back into its sheath. Am I not to drink the cup that the Father has given me?" (18:11). No such benign justification can be made for the many instances in which the Jews are portrayed as seeking Jesus' arrest and death.

Of course, not every act of violence stems from a perpetrator's hatred of a victim. It is unlikely, for example, that Jesus hated the individual merchants and money-changers whom he tossed out of the temple, or that Peter personally hated poor Malchus, the servant of the high priest. But according to this Gospel, the Jews' violence toward Jesus *is* directly motivated by hatred. In 15:24, Jesus tells his followers, "If I had not done among them the works that no one else did, they would not have sin. But

now they have seen and hated both me and my Father." Even with the use
of personal pronouns ("they") rather than nouns ("Jews"), it is clear that
Jesus is talking of the Jews. Any lingering doubt is dispelled by the following verse, in which Jesus explains that their violence fulfills "the word that
is written in their law, 'They hated me without a cause'"(15:25; cf. Ps
35:19, 69:5). Thus the grammar of violence in the Gospel of John is also a
grammar of hate. The Jews hate Jesus and ultimately kill him. Jesus is the
victim; the Jews are the perpetrators.

The story we have just summarized tells what we might call a "historical tale" in that it situates Jesus within a specific historical place and time.
The place is Roman Palestine. The time is the early first century, when
Pontius Pilate ruled over Judea on Rome's behalf, some decades prior to
the Jewish revolt against Rome of 66–70 C.E. But this is not the only story
that the Fourth Gospel tells. Probing beneath the story's surface reveals
two other, more subtle narratives, each of which parallels and intersects
the others in a variety of ways. In the shadows of the historical tale,
according to many scholars, lurks a second story, that of the "Johannine
community." This story may be called the "ecclesiological tale," from the
Greek word ἐκκλησία, meaning assembly, gathering, or later, church. The
Fourth Gospel nowhere uses the word ἐκκλησία; it does not prophecy the
founding of a community, as does Matt 16:18, or spell out the rules and
principles that should govern such a community, as do the letters of Paul.
There are no archaeological remains of this Johannine community nor are
there any explicit references to such a group in any ancient sources.[5] Nevertheless, the very nature of this Gospel, with its distinctive story line and
theology, implies the existence of a community within which and for
which the Gospel would have been written. Between the lines we may dis-
cern some of the problems of this community as it struggled to establish
and define itself within the religious and political spectrum of the Greco-
Roman world.

The Johannine Jesus has several things to say about the fate of his followers that may pertain not merely to the time of Jesus but also beyond
his death. These words seem to address a specific community and its experiences during the period in which the Gospel was written. In the farewell
discourses, Jesus prophesies the future persecution of his followers. He
adjures his audience to "Remember the word that I said to you, 'Servants
are not greater than their master.' If they persecuted me, they will persecute you; if they kept my word, they will keep yours also. But they will do
all these things to you on account of my name, because they do not know

him who sent me. If I had not come and spoken to them, they would not have sin; but now they have no excuse for their sin" (15:20–22). This prophecy is even more explicit in 16:2, in which Jesus proclaims: "They will put you out of the synagogues. Indeed, an hour is coming when those who kill you will think that by doing so they are offering worship to God. And they will do this because they have not known the Father or me" (16:2–3).

These statements exhibit a grammar of violence similar to the one that is apparent in the historical tale. The subject is again the Jews, and the verbs express violent behavior. But these statements now reach beyond the time frame of Jesus' life to a future persecution of his followers. Here the object of the Jews' violence is not Jesus but the group that continued to believe in him after his death. The simple grammar of hate that pertained in Jesus' lifetime is thus carried over into the experience of the community.

The third narrative level of this Gospel is a "cosmological tale" that provides the broad chronological, geographical, and theological framework within which the historical tale is placed. The cosmological tale has the cosmos—or the entire universe—as its setting, and eternity as its time frame. Its hero is the preexistent Word who becomes flesh and is sent into the world to bring salvation (1:1–18; 3:16). Its villain is the "ruler of this world" (14:30), "the evil one" (17:15), Satan (13:27), or the devil (8:44, 13:2). Its plot describes the origin of the hero in the divine realm, his descent into the world, his mission to humankind, his defeat of the "ruler of this world," and his return to the Father.[6]

The cosmological tale also revolves around love, hate, and violence, but these emotions and actions are expressed in more complex and less direct ways than in the other two tales. Just as the relatively simple love/hate relationships in the historical and ecclesiological tales emerge through relatively simple grammatical structures (Jews hate/kill Jesus/ followers), so do the more complex relationships in the cosmological tale appear in the more complex grammatical structures with which this Gospel portrays Jesus' universal salvific role.

Two examples will illustrate this complexity. In John 3:18, Jesus declares, "Those who believe in him are not condemned; but those who do not believe are condemned already, because they have not believed in the name of the only Son of God." This sentence has two clauses. In the first clause, the subject is "those who believe in him" and the verb is "are not condemned." The verb is passive, indicating that the agent of the action ("to condemn") is unnamed; the subject of the sentence is the one who experiences rather than perpetrates the action of condemnation. The potential of violence (condemnation) exists but is not realized because of the subject's positive faith stance toward Jesus.

The second clause reverses the first. The subject is "those who do not believe." The verb ("are condemned") is again passive. The subordinate clause ("because they have not believed in the name of the only Son of God") reiterates and emphasizes the identity of the subject as nonbelievers in Jesus. This formulation signals a move out of the historical plane, in which specific group and individual characters are identified, and into the cosmological level, in which large cosmic forces are at work. But the two levels are connected; we know that "those who do not believe" are the Jews, since they are amply identified in these terms elsewhere in the Gospel (for example, 8:45). The agent of condemnation, though unspecified, is certainly divine.

This identification is made explicit in the second example. In 3:36, Jesus, or perhaps the narrator,[7] declares, "Whoever believes in the Son has eternal life; whoever disobeys the Son will not see life, but must endure God's wrath." The subject of the second clause is "whoever disobeys the son." One of its verbs is "will not see" and its direct object is "life." The second verb is "must endure" and its object is the "wrath of God." Here the violence is expressed indirectly in the second clause; not seeing life is surely the equivalent of "seeing death." Also in the second clause, the notion of not seeing life is defined as enduring God's wrath. The import of this grammatical structure becomes clearer if one transposes the passive verbs into active ones. Thus the statements above might read: God (the subject) condemns those who do not believe (object).

In reading the cosmological and historical levels together, then, it is clear that the cosmological tale reverses the grammatical, and thereby also the theological, relationships that are set out in the historical and ecclesiological tales. Furthermore, the actions and events in the historical and ecclesiological tales have repercussions in the cosmological tale. In the historical tale, the Jews kill Jesus. In the cosmological tale, Jesus/God condemn the Jews to death precisely because they strive to kill Jesus. As we have already seen, the historical tale attributes the Jews' violence to their hatred, that is, their failure to believe in Jesus. In the cosmological tale, their hatred results in their being condemned to the enduring wrath of God.

Implicit in the expectation of condemnation is the notion of judgment. Just as the Jews have judged that Jesus deserves to die according to their

law (19:7), so do God and Jesus judge that the Jews deserve eternal condemnation. Jesus says in 12:47–49: "I do not judge anyone who hears my
words and does not keep them, for I came not to judge the world, but to
save the world. The one who rejects me and does not receive my word has
a judge; on the last day the word that I have spoken will serve as judge, for
I have not spoken on my own, but the Father who sent me has himself giv-
en me a commandment about what to say and what to speak." Not only
does the divine word (and Word) condemn them, but so also does the
Jews' own, divinely given law, the Torah. "Do not think that I will accuse
you before the Father; your accuser is Moses, on whom you have set your
hope. If you believed Moses, you would believe me, for he wrote about
me. But if you do not believe what he wrote, how will you believe what I
say?" (5:45–47).

The Jews' acts of persecution in the historical and ecclesiological tales
take place on an earthly, physical plane. While it may seem that the Jews,
on an earthly level, succeed in vanquishing their foe, their comeuppance in
the fullness of time is divinely guaranteed. God's condemnation of the
Jews may not be visible on an earthly level, but it has eternal consequences. In 5:28, this condemnation is prophesied for the future but
imminent time of universal resurrection. Jesus warns: "Do not be aston-
ished at this; for the hour is coming when all who are in their graves will
hear his voice and will come out—those who have done good, to the resurrection of life, and those who have done evil, to the resurrection of condemnation" (5:28–29). The linking of judgment and condemnation to
death is made explicit in 8:23–24, in which Jesus tells the Jews, "You are
from below, I am from above; you are of this world, I am not of this
world. I told you that you would die in your sins, for you will die in your
sins unless you believe that I am he."

But the cosmological tale goes beyond merely condemning the Jews. If
in the ecclesiological tale the Jews expel believers from the synagogue
(16:2), in the cosmological tale, God, through Jesus, expels Jews from the
eternal covenant with him. This expulsion is effected in John 8:31–59, the
discourse that provides the immediate context for Jesus' accusation that
the Jews have the devil as their father (8:44).

John 8:31–59 recounts a confrontation between Jesus and a group of
Jews who had believed in him but apparently no longer do so (8:31). The
discussion revolves precisely around their irreconcilable interpretations of
the covenantal relationship between the Jews and God. The Jews' self-
identity is grounded in the notion of election, according to which God has

chosen them as his special people. This covenantal relationship is governed by mutual love and obligation, and is sealed in the Torah, God's gift to the Jewish people, the revelation of his will, and the way of life that Jews are bound by their covenantal promises to follow and obey. Jesus, by contrast, argues vigorously that at this moment in history, God has redrawn the rules by sending his Son into the world as an expression of his love (3:16); in this new reality, covenantal relationship with God belongs only to those who believe that Jesus is truly God's son and the Messiah of Israel (20:30–31).

The Jews' brief comments in John 8 assert their covenantal relationship with God by emphasizing three key points: that Abraham is their father (8:33, 39), that they have never served or been enslaved to anyone or anything (8:33), and that they are children of God (8:41). Together, these elements proclaim the Jews' profound commitment to monotheism, a tenet that is central in the Hebrew Bible, Jewish theology, and Jewish liturgy.[8] In claiming to be children of Abraham, the Jews draw attention to Abraham's status as the patriarch of the Jewish people. As the first monotheist, Abraham is known in Jewish tradition as the first person to recognize the one God as the creator of the world.[9] The Jews are Abraham's children insofar as they too maintain a firm commitment to monotheism. The Jews' claim that they have never served or been enslaved to anyone is more ambiguous. In a literal sense, the Jews certainly were once enslaved, in Egypt under the pharaohs. But the verb normally translated "to be enslaved" has another, well-established meaning, namely, "to serve," as in, to serve many gods.[10] The Jews' boast that they have never "served" anyone or anything (8:33) is thus another expression of their monotheism. Indeed, to serve another "divine" being—such as Jesus claims to be—would be tantamount to slavery. Finally, the Jews' covenantal relationship with God bestows upon them the status of God's children. In Exod 4:22–23, for example, God coaches Moses on what to say to Pharaoh as he tries to secure Israel's release from slavery: "Then you shall say to Pharaoh, 'Thus says the LORD: Israel is my firstborn son. . . . Let my son go that he may worship me.'" Thus the Jews' three major claims—that they are children of Abraham, have never served any other beings, and that they are children of God—all make the same point: Jews are in an eternal covenantal relationship with God.

The Johannine Jesus, in turn, insists that the Jews can no longer lay claim to this special relationship. For Jesus, the Jews' rejection of his messiahship proves that they cannot be the children of Abraham. Whereas

Abraham accepted God's messengers (cf. Gen 18), the Jews try to kill God's son (8:40). Despite their boasts to the contrary, the Jews were and continue to be enslaved as long as they refuse to believe. In 8:34–36, Jesus proclaims: "Everyone who commits sin is a slave to sin. The slave does not have a permanent place in the household; the son has a place there forever. So if the Son makes you free, you will be free indeed." Finally, the Jews cannot be the children of God: "If God were your Father, you would love me, for I came from God and now I am here. I did not come on my own, but he sent me" (8:42). The Jews' rejection of Jesus has ousted them from their covenantal relationship with God, and, so Jesus asserts, has revealed their true ancestry as children of the devil: "You are from your father the devil, and you choose to do your father's desires" (8:44). In John 8, the Fourth Evangelist claims that the new covenant mediated through Jesus supersedes the covenant established on Mount Sinai with the giving of the Torah. The Jews' disbelief expels the Jews from the covenant with God, that is, from the group that benefits from close and exclusive relationship with God, and puts them in the devil's league.

The notion of expulsion or exclusion from the divine covenant appears in a number of different metaphors throughout the Gospel. In John 10:25–28, Jesus tells the Jews that they do not believe because they do not belong to his sheep. "My sheep hear my voice. I know them, and they follow me. I give them eternal life, and they will never perish" (10:27–28). John 15 employs the image of the vine branch. Jesus declares: "I am the true vine, and my Father is the vine grower. He removes every branch in me that bears no fruit. Every branch that bears fruit he prunes to make it bear more fruit. . . . Whoever does not abide in me is thrown away like a branch and withers; such branches are gathered, thrown into the fire, and burned" (15:1–6).

The Jews' rejection of Jesus not only results in their expulsion from the divine covenant but it also severs their ties to the temple, God's house. This consequence is intimated in John 8:35, when Jesus declares: "The slave does not have a permanent place in the household; the son has a place there forever." Because the Jews have rejected God's son, they remain slaves to sin, and thereby relinquish their right to God's house. This is illustrated in John 2:16, when Jesus drives the merchants and money-changers out of the temple and shouts: "Take these things out of here! Stop making my Father's house a marketplace!"

Earlier we described this scene as one instance in which the simple grammar of hate and violence (Jews/kill/Jesus) is reversed (Jesus/expels/

merchants). In the context of the historical tale, this event is not clearly understood either by the Jews, who question Jesus about it, or by the disciples (2:18, 22). Only after his death is its import clear. By cleansing the temple, Jesus prophecies that the Jews will destroy his temple, namely, his body (2:21). As a consequence of this act, they fall out of divine favor, and hence must be expelled from the temple. True, Jesus does not expel everyone, only the merchants and the money-changers. But he is not simply declaring that commerce has no place in the temple. Rather, he is symbolically expelling the entire sacrificial system of divine worship as mandated by the Torah. This system is undermined when pilgrims are unable to exchange their currency and to buy animals fit for sacrifice. In cleansing the temple, Jesus is identifying the temple with his own body as God's new abode. As God's Son, Jesus is the place where God's presence now abides.

The cosmological level of the Gospel narrative provides the most basic and fundamental context for the apparent love/hate contradiction with which we began. The love that should characterize the relationship among Jesus' followers is called a "new commandment" and is based on the love between God and Jesus on the one hand and between Jesus and his followers on the other hand. Through the cosmological tale, this new commandment sets out a new covenantal relationship, a new way of relating to God, that supplants the old covenant, as epitomized in the "old commandment," that is, the Torah. The old commandment commands the Jews to love God (Deut 6:4–6) and proclaims in turn God's love for Israel (Exod 15:13; cf. Isa 57:8, 10; Joel 2:13). But Jesus' coming adds a new condition to this covenant, for obedience to God's will no longer requires obedience to the Torah's rules but rather faith in God's son. To have faith in God's son is to love him, and by extension, to love and be loved by God the Father. The love commandment in Jesus' farewell discourses, according to the Fourth Gospel, is not the universally appealing and universally accepting attitude and emotion that it might seem to be when taken out of its literary and theological context in the Gospel as a whole. Rather, it is explicitly limited to the circle of Jesus' faithful followers.

The grammar of hate, according to which Jews hate and kill Jesus and his followers and in turn are hated and killed by Jesus and by God, drives a sharp wedge between the nonbelieving Jews and those who are bound by Jesus' new gospel of love. How does one explain this state of affairs? On the one hand, one could argue that the perceived Jewish role in the historical tale—as Jesus' persecutors and murderers—is enough to account for and, perhaps, to warrant the anti-Jewish language in the Gospel and the strong emotions that underlie it. Certainly many Christians through the centuries, including John Chrysostom in the fourth century and Martin Luther in the sixteenth century, thought so.[11]

Modern historians, on the other hand, look beyond the events of Jesus' life and death to the situation and experiences of the early Christian community in relationship to the Jews. Many scholars argue that the ecclesiological tale is not merely a narrative layer within the literary text that is the Fourth Gospel, but rather that it also reflects the real life situation of the Johannine community at the end of the first century C.E.[12] In this view, Jesus' prophecies about the Jews' persecution of his followers in fact describe a specific historical experience in which the Jews really did persecute the Johannine Christians, namely, a Jewish expulsion of Johannine Christians from the synagogue. Three passages in the Gospel of John are thought to relate to such an expulsion. In John 9, Jesus heals a man born blind. The Jews interrogate his parents and ask them what had happened to their son. They deflect the question, as the narrator tells us, "because they were afraid of the Jews; for the Jews had already agreed that anyone who confessed Jesus to be the Messiah would be put out of the synagogue" (9:22). Because expulsion from the synagogue is implausible in Jesus' own day, this statement is thought to refer to either a localized or more general policy of expulsion that the Johannine community itself experienced due to its confession of Jesus as the Christ. A similar reality is thought to be reflected in John 12:42, in which the narrator declares that "many, even of the authorities, believed in him. But because of the Pharisees they did not confess it, for fear that they would be put out of the synagogue." Finally, John 16:2 prophecies a time when Jews will persecute believers and put them out of the synagogue, and even kill them. On the basis of these passages, some scholars suggest that the negative depictions of Jews and Judaism in the Gospel, including 8:44 and the condemnation of the Jews to divine wrath, are the community's response to the experience of exclusion from the synagogue.[13] This position is problematic. First, there is no external evidence to support the claim that Jews excluded any groups from the synagogue in the late first century.[14] Second, to suggest that the Gospel's difficult language about the Jews is a justifiable response to the experience of persecution is to hold the Jews themselves responsible for its presence in the Gospel text.[15]

The cosmological tale suggests another solution. Whatever the details of the historical relationship between Johannine Christians and the Jewish community, the former were likely profoundly disappointed at the overall

lack of acceptance of their message among the Jews to whom the Gospel
was first preached. As a minor Jewish sect in Roman Palestine in the late
first century C.E., Christians were powerless to act against the Jews on the
historical plane. But Christians could take full cosmological vengeance by
proclaiming Jews' exclusion from God's covenant and prophesying their
future, eternal, destruction. Jesus himself suggests as much in his exchange
with Pilate, in 18:36–37. When Pilate asks whether Jesus is really a king,
Jesus answers, "My kingdom is not from this world. If my kingdom were
from this world, my followers would be fighting to keep me from being
handed over to the Jews. But as it is, my kingdom is not from here." Pilate
then asks again: "So you are a king?" Jesus answers, "You say that I am a
king. For this I was born, and for this I came into the world, to testify to
the truth. Everyone who belongs to the truth listens to my voice." In other words, Jesus is a king in the cosmological, nonworldly sense; his subjects are all those who listen to his voice. This cosmological kingdom does
not allow the bearing of arms, as does the earthly kingdom of which Pilate
is currently the representative. But the Gospel preaches that Jesus' kingdom is ultimately more powerful, more enduring, and more violent by
virtue of its divine mandate and its cosmic scope.

The Fourth Gospel, written in a context of Christian powerlessness,
contented itself with the eternal damnation of the unbelieving Jews. Some
later Christians, however, did not hesitate to call for their physical death
as well. Indeed, in the late fourth century, we find such writers as John
Chrysostom calling explicitly for the death of the Jews. "Although such
beasts are unfit for work, they are fit for killing. And this is what happened to the Jews: while they were making themselves unfit for work, they
grew fit for slaughter. This is why Christ said: 'But as for these my enemies, who did not want me to be king over them, bring them here and slay
them'" (Luke 19:27).[16]

Much had changed by Chrysostom's time. Christianity had become the
state religion of the Roman Empire; most Christians had Gentile and not
Jewish origins. Chrysostom may or may not have intended that Christians
should literally slaughter Jews. Many others, however, in Roman,
medieval, and modern Europe did tolerate and even encourage the persecution and killing of Jews, acts often justified by the charge of deicide and
accompanied by the image of the Jew as devil. The Gospel of John is not
solely responsible for this sad, shared history.[17] But the persistence of its
imagery shows that the grammar of violence, and the discourses of love
and hate, can leap from a literary text and into the annals of history

whether they were intended to do so or not. This is a lesson we would do well to remember, as we listen to the grammar and the discourses that swirl around us in the troubled world that we ourselves live in today.

Notes

1. For example, see the websites at http://www.restorationministry.com/tracts/the_gospel_of_love.htm; www.ccel.org/s/schaff/hcc1/htm/i.XI.72.htm.

2. One of the earliest sketches is from the Forest Roll of Essex, dated 1277, bearing the superscription "Aaron, son of the devil." Joshua Trachtenberg, *The Devil and the Jews: The Medieval Conception of the Jew and Its Relation to Modern Anti-Semitism* (New Haven, Conn.: Yale University Press, 1943), 26.

3. "Certainly the Jew is the very devil incarnal." *The Merchant of Venice* (II.ii.27).

4. Numerous anti-Semitic sites can be uncovered simply by doing a Google search for the words "Jew devil."

5. The community is more directly discernible in the letters of John, which are generally considered to have been written within the same circle, and possibly by the same author, as the Fourth Gospel. Cf. Raymond E. Brown, *The Community of the Beloved Disciple: The Life, Loves, and Hates of an Individual Church in New Testament Times* (London: G. Chapman, 1979).

6. The three levels are discussed in detail in Adele Reinhartz, *The Word in the World: The Cosmological Tale in the Fourth Gospel* (Atlanta: SBL 1992), and in idem, *Befriending the Beloved Disciple: A Jewish Reading of the Gospel of John* (New York: Continuum, 2001).

7. The context makes it difficult to determine the boundary between Jesus' discourse and the narrator's commentary. For discussion of this perennial crux, see Raymond E. Brown, *The Gospel According to John, I–XII* (Anchor Bible 29; Garden City, N.Y.: Doubleday, 1966), 159–60.

8. Cf. Deut 6:4–6: "Hear, O Israel, the LORD our God the LORD is One." The opening section of the Decalogue (Exod 20:2–3) declares God's uniqueness and singularity: "I am the LORD your God, who brought you out of the land of Egypt, out of the house of slavery; you shall have no other gods before me. You shall not make for yourself an idol, whether in the form of anything that is in heaven above, or that is on the earth beneath, or that is in the water under the earth. You shall not bow down to them or worship them." Both of these texts assert God's uniqueness and call upon Israel to worship God alone.

9. Cf. *Apoc. Ab.* 1, *Jub.* 12.12–14.

10. In many places in the Septuagint (a Greek translation of the Hebrew Bible from the second century B.C.E.), this verb specifically refers to worship of God or gods. For example, Ps 106:36 accuses the Israelites of being ensnared by the idols whom they served. In his letter to the Galatians, Paul uses this verb in a way that implies both worship and slavery (Gal 4:9; cf. Jer 5:19). He chastises the Galatians, who are of Gentile background, by asking, "Now, however, that you have come to know God, or rather to

be known by God, how can you turn back again to the weak and beggarly elemental spirits? How can you want to be enslaved to them again?"

11. Cf. Robert L. Wilken, *John Chrysostom and the Jews: Rhetoric and Reality in the Late Fourth Century* (Berkeley: University of California Press, 1983), 125–26; Martin Luther, *The Jews and Their Lies* (Marietta, Ga.: Thunderbolt Press, 1900).

12. See, for example, J. L. Martyn, *History and Theology in the Fourth Gospel* (2d ed.; Nashville: Abingdon, 1979).

13. See discussion in Robert Kysar, "The Promises and Perils of Preaching on the Gospel of John," *Dialog* 19, no. 3 (1980): 219.

14. The definitive critique of this hypothesis was made by Reuven Kimelman, "*Birkat Ha-Minim* and the Lack of Evidence for an Anti-Christian Jewish Prayer in Late Antiquity," in *Jewish and Christian Self-Definition* (ed. E. P. Sanders; Philadelphia: Fortress Press, 1981), 2.226–44, 2.391–403.

15. See Adele Reinhartz, "The Johannine Community and Its Jewish Neighbors: A Reappraisal," in *What is John? Vol. II: Literary and Social Readings of the Fourth Gospel* (ed. Fernando F. Segovia; Atlanta: Scholars Press, 1998), 111–38; and idem, *Befriending the Beloved Disciple,* passim.

16. St. John Chrysostom, *Discourses Against Judaizing Christians,* I.ii.6 (trans. Paul W. Harkins; vol. 68 of *The Fathers of the Church*; Washington, D.C.: The Catholic University of America Press, 1979), 8.

17. The role of Christianity in the origins and history of anti-Semitism is assessed differently by different historians. See Judith Taylor Gold, *Monsters and Madonnas: The Roots of Christian Anti-Semitism* (New York: New Amsterdam, 1988); James Carroll, *Constantine's Sword: The Church and the Jews: A History* (Boston: Houghton Mifflin, 2001); Rosemary Radford Ruether, *Faith and Fratricide: The Theological Roots of Anti-Semitism* (New York: Seabury Press, 1974); Carol Rittner et al., ed., *The Holocaust and the Christian World: Reflections on the Past, Challenges for the Future* (New York: Continuum, 2000); John G. Gager, *The Origins of Anti-Semitism: Attitudes toward Judaism in Pagan and Christian Antiquity* (New York: Oxford University Press, 1983); Lionel B. Steiman, *Paths to Genocide: Antisemitism in Western History* (New York: St. Martin's Press, 1998); John Dominic Crossan, *Who Killed Jesus?: Exposing the Roots of Anti-Semitism in the Gospel Story of the Death of Jesus* (San Francisco: HarperSanFrancisco, 1996).

7

The Need for the
Stoning of Stephen
SHELLY MATTHEWS

"The perfect martyr" (ὁ τέλειος μάρτυς) is the epithet given to Stephen in the conclusion to the early Christian narrative of the martyrs of Vienne and Lyons (Eusebius, *Hist. eccl.* 5.2.5). This essay argues that the narrative of the stoning of Stephen in Acts 6:8–8:1 does indeed depict a perfect martyr—one perfectly suited, that is, to Luke's rhetorical purposes in the two-volume work now known as the Gospel of Luke and the Acts of the Apostles.[1] In this work Luke constructs for followers of "the Way" a genealogy reaching back into Israelite traditions, and a sociology that drives a wedge between them and their Jewish contemporaries. One means by which Acts constructs a divide between "the Way" and "the Jews" is to portray the former as compatible, and the latter as incompatible, with Roman juridical ideals.[2] While ecclesial traditions of Jesus' death under Pontius Pilate and Paul's death in Rome posed a potential fault line in this construction, the killing of Stephen is an episode that is free from Roman juridical involvement. In Luke's telling, the death of Stephen through a stoning carried out by an unruly mob underscores Jewish barbarity, creates a breach between the church and the Jews, and brackets Romans out of the originary violence that produced the church's first martyred follower of Jesus and marked its first great expansion.

Because the story fits precisely into Luke's rhetorical design for his narrative of Christian origins, and because there are no extant witnesses to Stephen's martyrdom outside of the book of Acts until the time of Irenaeus, who apparently relies on Acts for his information, this essay further suggests that the very historicity of Stephen's murder itself should be called into question. As the argument here will show, the

Stephen narrative falls far short of two long-standing criteria of historicity used in Jesus research—dissimilarity and multiple attestation. Yet, in New Testament scholarship the kernel of the story, Stephen's murder by the Jewish mob, is regarded as incontrovertible history. Both the myth of the stoning of Stephen created by Luke and the unreflective certainty about its historicity among biblical scholars need to be interrogated in view of the hydra-headed phenomenon of ancient Christian anti-Judaism. Scholars concerned with the issue of Christian anti-Judaism must consider the effects of Luke's story, in which he constructs a Christian origin and essence that is innocent and violated over and against a Jewish essence that is violent and culpable. As with many New Testament texts, the story of the stoning of Stephen is one in which the violence *in* the text (Jews murdering a Christian) displaces the violence *of* the text (a Christian vilifying Jews).

Jesus—Stephen—Paul in Lukan Narrative and in Historical Reconstruction

In the narrative structure of Luke-Acts the story of Stephen functions as a bridge between the narratives of Jesus' passion and the trial of Paul. In broad general terms, the lives of all three persons conform to the Deuteronomistic pattern of the suffering prophet. All three are sent by God to deliver prophetic oracles, all are rejected by Israel, all suffer persecution in Jerusalem.[3] This pattern of the persecuted prophet is fleshed out through paralleled narrative details linking Stephen to Jesus: like Jesus, Stephen is brought before the Sanhedrin (Luke 22:26; cf. Acts 6:12); both Jesus and Stephen speak of the eschatological Son of Man at the right hand of God (Luke 22:69; cf. Acts 7:56); as Jesus commends his spirit to God on the cross (Luke 23:46), so Stephen prays to the Lord Jesus to receive his spirit at death (Acts 7:59).[4] Overlap between the passion narratives of Mark and Matthew and the Stephen narrative also suggest that Jesus' passion is a model for the death of Stephen. The charge common to Mark and Matthew concerning the destruction of the temple is not leveled against Jesus in the third gospel; rather, Luke reserves this accusation for the trial of Stephen (Mark 14:58; Matt 26:61; Acts 6:14; *not* in Luke).[5] This is also true of the charge of blasphemy (Mark 14:64; Matt 26:65; Acts 6:11; *not* in Luke) and the characterization of the accusers as false witnesses (Mark 14:56–57; Matt 26:60–61; Acts 6:13; *not* in Luke).

The linkage between Stephen and Paul in Acts is explicit. In an interjection devoid of subtlety, Luke introduces Paul at the moment of Stephen's death: "And dragging him outside of the city, they stoned him; laying their garments at the feet of a youth named Saul" (7:58); "And Saul approved of their killing him" (8:1a). Again in Paul's defense speech on the steps of the temple, Luke underscores the connection between Paul's own mission and Stephen's death. Observe the complex narrative construction in 22:17–21, a speech in which Paul narrates a past conversation between himself and the Lord, in which he has reminded the Lord specifically of the details implicating him in the death of Stephen, first mentioned in 7:58 and 8:1: "And I [Paul] said, 'Lord, they themselves know that I imprisoned and beat in the synagogues those believing in you, and when the blood of Stephen your martyr was shed I myself was standing by, approving and keeping the coats of those who killed him.'"

Stephen is also linked to Paul by the nearly identical wording of the charges leveled against them. In Acts 6:13, Stephen is accused of defying the temple: "This man never stops saying things against this holy place and the law," words mirrored in the accusation against Paul in Acts 21:28: "This is the man who is teaching everyone everywhere against our people, our law, and this place [the temple]."

Since the work of F. C. Baur in the nineteenth century, scholars mining Luke-Acts for historical details have understood Stephen to serve a bridging function in actual Christian history. Stephen, the historical person, has been seen as the crux of the link between the historical Jesus and the Apostle Paul. For Baur, and for many reading after him, the tie that has been understood to bind these three historical persons is their common anti-cultic, anti-ritual theologies.[6] In understanding Stephen as the hinge in this historical connection, the numerous literary links considered above have been dismissed as Lukan fabrication. Instead scholars have relied heavily on the accusations against Stephen in 6:11–14, which are deemed to reflect historical data. Here Stephen is charged with speaking against the law of Moses and the temple.[7] The long defense speech of 7:2–53 is also understood to contain traces of the historical Stephen's radical anti-temple critique (esp. 7:47–50).[8] Once the historical Stephen's theology is established as anti-law and anti-temple, it becomes but a short move to account for his death on these same theological grounds. As Helmut Koester observes, "Stephen was martyred, not because he was a Christian, but because as a Christian he rejected the law and ritual of his Jewish past."[9]

These anti-cultic and anti-ritual reconstructions of Stephen, which have always had detractors,[10] are currently being called into question in view of our understanding of the nineteenth-century orientalist binary that governed Baur's and many subsequent authors' reconstructions of Stephen and the Hellenists. In that century, Stephen and especially Paul were cast as Western, Hellenist, Christian heroes who freed the "spiritual" gospel from its Eastern, Hebrew, "fleshy" fetters. So, for example, J. B. Lightfoot hails Stephen as "a champion of emancipation . . . the first to 'look steadfastly to the end of that which is abolished,' to sound the death-knell of Mosaic ordinances and the temple worship, and to claim for the Gospel unfettered liberty and universal rights."[11] Scholars with more appreciation of the place of cult and ritual in Hellenistic Judaism than Baur or Lightfoot now suggest that the historical Stephen could not have dismissed these practices so cavalierly, and that the divide between Jesus followers and other Jews could not have been so deep merely a generation after the crucifixion.[12] However, both camps of Stephen scholars—those seeing him as hostile and those seeing him as sympathetic to Jewish institutions—do share an important common interpretive assumption. With near unanimity, Stephen scholars assume that behind Luke's highly stylized narrative of Stephen there lies a historical person and a historical incident, a kernel of truth about the first murder of a Jesus follower by Jews.[13]

The Sure and Certain Murder of Stephen

Expressions of certainty about Stephen's historicity in nineteenth-century scholarship are emphatic. Those earliest of historical critics, heady with the enthusiasm of being free to question both the miraculous and the idealizing tendencies in Acts on rational grounds, chip away unrelentingly at the foundations of Acts as reliable history. But when they come upon the story of Stephen, they understand themselves to have hit bedrock. Thus F. C. Baur, while questioning the historicity of persecution against the earliest apostles in Acts, observes that "the martyrdom of Stephen and the persecution of the Christians which was connected with it, wears the indubitable stamp of historical reality."[14] Likewise, his son-in-law, Eduard Zeller, writes, "The death of Stephen is incontestably the clearest point in the history of Christianity prior to Paul. With this event we find ourselves for the first time on undeniably historical ground. It would be guaranteed even by the one decisive fact caused by the persecution of Stephen, the conversion of Paul; if indeed any further proof of its reality were required for an event so visibly involved in the development of the Christian cause."[15] One might smile at the quaintness of nineteenth-century historians asserting bedrock historicity without providing substantive rationale, but it is difficult to dismiss this same interpretive move as "quaint" when it is found in pages published at the end of the twentieth century as well.

Consider, for instance, the revised dissertation of Craig Hill, *Hellenists and Hebrews: Reappraising Division within the Earliest Church,* published in 1992. In it, Hill calls into question the fundamental distinctions of how the "Hellenists" and "Hebrews" in Acts are reconstructed in modern historiography. He argues that the persecution of Stephen and the Hellenists does *not* demonstrate their theological independence from the Hebrews. He throws into doubt the historicity of the "severe persecution" that Luke describes in 8:1b, and marvels at the way that many earlier scholars have tried to argue that only Gentile Christians, and *not* Jewish Christians, were affected by this violence. He deftly pulls the rug out from under arguments that Stephen is radically anti-temple and anti-ritual, pointing out that we have no reliable information about the beliefs of Stephen. However, the bedrock that was hit by F. C. Baur remains fixed, even in this work that styles itself as deconstructing Baur's foundations. Hill concludes his chapter on Stephen without ultimately calling into question the historicity of this narrative of originary violence. He writes, "*Apart from the fact of his martyrdom*, we can know almost nothing about Stephen; the account in Acts appears to have been composed of little more than a few pieces of traditional information."[16]

This sure and certain knowledge of the historicity of Stephen's martyrdom is particularly striking when one considers the rigorous methods of historical analysis that apply in Jesus research. Modeled so carefully on Jesus' death, and serving the function of distancing Christians from Jews, Luke's narrative of the death of Stephen does not pass the criterion of dissimilarity. Perhaps more to the point is how Stephen's martyrdom fails the criterion of multiple attestation. Before the time of Irenaeus, Stephen's death is attested only in the book of Acts.[17] I turn now to a discussion of the use of Stephen's martyrdom in the early church.

The Use of Stephen in the Early Church

Given the pivotal role that Luke grants to Stephen in Acts, it is striking that no other New Testament author mentions him. Although Paul and Luke both speak of figures such as Priscilla and Aquila, Apollos, and

Barnabas, no corroborating stories about Stephen exist in the Pauline corpus. As François Bovon, who assumes Stephen's historicity, observes, "The absence in the Pauline corpus is particularly surprising . . . the theological affinity between the two men should have urged the apostle to the nations to find strength in his memory of Stephen."[18]

While there are already references to a succession of martyrs in early and mid-second-century Christian literature, Stephen is not mentioned as part of this succession until the time of Irenaeus. Both Clement of Rome and Polycarp exhort imitation of earlier Christian martyrs. However, these two authors, who precede Irenaeus, have neither knowledge of the book of Acts, nor independent access to the Stephen tradition. Neither of them will push the chain of Christian martyrs from his own time back beyond the time of Paul. Clement cites the examples of the "pillars of the Church," Paul and Peter, who were "persecuted and contended unto death," due to "jealousy and envy" (1 Clem. 5.1–6.2). Polycarp's chain of martyrs goes no further than "Paul and the other Apostles" (*Phil* 9.1–2). In Irenaeus's *Against Heresies,* for the first time outside of Acts, Stephen is given the status of primacy among Christian martyrs.[19] He is "the first to follow the footsteps of the martyrdom of the Lord, being the first that was slain for confessing Christ, speaking boldly among the people and teaching them. . . ." (*Haer.* 3.12.10 [*ANF:* 434]; cf. 4.15.1). Stephen's speech is cited in *Against Heresies* as an authoritative witness to the orthodox past that Irenaeus constructs. Also in martyr acts dated no earlier than Irenaeus, Stephen is cited as the exemplary model. Eusebius preserves the Letter of the Churches of Vienne and Lyon, which is generally dated to a period not long after the persecution of 177 C.E., and which some attribute to Irenaeus. In it the martyrs are said to have "prayed for those who had inflicted torture, even as did Stephen, the perfect martyr" (Eusebius, *Hist. eccl.* 5.2.5). Tertullian pairs Stephen and Isaiah as examples of "patient" martyrs (*Pat.* 14.1).[20] Stephen's final prayer before death, "Lord Jesus receive my spirit," also enters the tradition no earlier than this time (cf. *Acta Carpi,* Latin recension, 4.6; *Passio Pionii* 21.9; *Acta Iulii Veterani* 4.4).

After Irenaeus, the most detailed comment on Stephen's death and its significance is in Eusebius's recapitulation of Acts. Eusebius sees the martyrdom of Stephen as a turning point in history, an originary act of violence, dividing the church from the Jews: "On the martyrdom of Stephen there arose the first and greatest persecution of the Church in Jerusalem by the Jews" (*Hist. eccl.* 2.1.8).[21] Throughout the history of interpretation of the book of Acts, Eusebius remains by and large unchallenged on this

point. At the end of the nineteenth century, J. B. Lightfoot captured both
the originary and the violent implications of this story most succinctly
through the utilization of sacramental language. He writes, "the Church
of the Gentiles was baptized in the blood of Stephen."[22]

Two elements of Eusebius's commentary on Stephen that are generally
not observed by historical critics should be considered here. Eusebius
mentions how purposeful Stephen's death is: "Stephen was first after his
Lord not only in ordination, but, as though he had been put forward for
this very purpose [ὥσπερ εἰς αὐτὸ τοῦτο προαχθείς], also in that he was
stoned to death by the Lord's murderers" (*Hist. eccl.* 2.1.1). While Eusebius undoubtedly would attribute such purposefulness to providence, I
would highlight again how perfectly suited Stephen's death is to Luke's
own purposes. Likewise, Eusebius recognizes the symbolism of the Greek
"stephanos," mentioning how the name befits "the first to carry off the
crown . . . which was gained by the martyrs of Christ found worthy of
victory" (*Hist. eccl.* 2.1.1). While I observe with Eusebius the significance
of the symbolic name, again I suggest this is Luke's hand, and not the
hand of providence in history at work. I turn now to a discussion of the
way in which Stephen functions as Luke's "perfect martyr."

Luke, Stephen, and Imperial Sociology

A key reason reconstructions of the historical Stephen's theology are con-
troverted is that Luke's primary interest in 6:8–8:1 has little to do with
crediting Stephen with a particular set of "beliefs." In the story of the
stoning of Stephen, as in the book of Acts as a whole, Luke is less concerned with detailing theological differences between Jews and followers
of the Way on matters of law and ritual—consider his depiction of Paul as
believing "everything laid down according to the law or written in the
prophets" (Acts 24:14)—than with deriding juridical processes and social
behaviors of Jews vis-à-vis followers of the Way. For example, Luke's
adaptation of Mark's passion narrative in his own gospel is governed not
by his theological concerns, but rather by concern to present the juridical
process of Romans as fair, and that of Jews as unfair.[23] In the arrest of
Paul as narrated in Acts 21:27–22:30, the Roman tribune takes great
pains to find out the "truth" about Paul, while the Jewish mob attempts
to kill him.[24]

In an important essay on the Jews in Acts, Lawrence Wills observes
the influence of what he calls "imperial sociology" on Luke's portrayal of

violent Jewish mob scenes. That is, historians of the Roman imperial peri-od such as Tacitus, Sallust, and Josephus tend to depict the masses, whom they fear and despise, as easily incited by base and dishonest compatriots to acts of violent rebellion.[25] Luke adopts the perspective of imperial soci-ology in his depiction of the Jews in Acts by repeatedly demonstrating their resort to mob violence when faced with missionaries of "the Way" (cf. 13:44–50; 14:1–6; 14:19; 17:5–6; 18:12–17; 21:17–31; 23:10; 23:20–21). Wills's conclusion is worth quoting in full:

> The narrative method in Acts in regards to the Jews is not to state the salvation-history dogma that their theology makes them wrong and lost—although the author probably believes this—but to show that the Jews are every bit as disorderly and rebellious as one would expect from the fact that they were involved in three bloody rebel-lions in seventy years . . . what is disturbing about Luke's view of the Jews is that it is seen from the ruling Roman perspective, graph-ically and tendentiously realized in the Jewish mob scenes. Theolog-ical controversies no longer hold center stage, but the real issue is citizenship and acceptance in the Roman worldview."[26]

Recognizing Luke's dual interests in denigrating Jewish legal processes and depicting Jews as fomenters of violence leads to the solution of the problem that Luke's narrative of Stephen's death contains both elements of a Jewish legal procedure and of mob violence. On the one hand, Stephen is brought before the Jewish legal council (Acts 6:12; Gk: *synedri-on*) and interrogated by the high priest (7:1), and formal witnesses observe his execution (7:58b); on the other hand, the procedure is instigated by firebrands who stoke up the crowd and incite false witnesses (6:9–11), and the "trial" is interrupted by an angered mob that drags him out of the city to be stoned (7:58a). For most historical critics, one set of details—those concerning the lynch mob—is judged to have historical value, while the other set—the legal proceedings—is understood to have been added by Luke.[27] In Ernst Haenchen's vivid rendering of this scenario, Luke is presented as gripping his framework tightly and attempting to steer his account in the direction of a court proceeding, while his lynch-mob source threatens to overtake him and destroy his framing enterprise altogether.[28] Rather than positing an author who is trying desperately to frame his unwieldy source, I suggest that Luke is quite in control of this narrative, and that the easy alteration between legal procedure and mob violence is precisely the point: Jewish legal procedure is so basely inferior to Roman jurisprudence that it cannot but devolve into savage mob behavior. The narrative functions both to underscore that Jews are prone to mob violence and to highlight the deficient legal processes of Jews.

Identifying Luke's pro-Roman and anti-Jewish tendencies under the rubrics of imperial sociology and jurisprudence also deepens the significance of Stephen's death by stoning in the following way. In contrast to the Lukan passion of Jesus and the trial of Paul in Acts, responsibility for Stephen's trial and death lies squarely and solely upon the Jews. That is, while Luke softens Roman involvement in Jesus' death by including Pilate's three-fold proclamation of Jesus' innocence, and by moving the Roman soldiers to a peripheral role in the crucifixion, he does not entirely ignore the early tradition that Jesus was subjected to the Roman punishment of crucifixion under Pontius Pilate. Likewise, while the arrest of Paul in Acts by the Roman soldiers is portrayed as a means of "rescuing" him from the Jews, and the tradition that Paul is martyred at the hands of the Romans receives no mention, Luke still concedes that Roman soldiers have arrested Paul, and he awaits trial under Roman surveillance. In contrast, the story of Stephen, for which Acts is the earliest extant witness, is Luke's perfectly "Roman-free" narrative of the murder of an early Christian.

Not only the identity of the actors as a mob of Jews, but also the means by which they kill Stephen, the stoning, is crucial to the import of the story. Death by stoning in the Hebrew Bible is generally prescribed for crimes perceived to have been inflicted on the community rather than on an individual. Thus J. J. Finkelstein writes, "Offenses which entail this mode of execution must . . . be of a character that, either in theory or in fact, 'offend' the corporate community or are believed to compromise its most cherished values to the degree that the commission of the offense places the community itself in jeopardy."[29] Because the entire community is offended, "all hands" in the community take part in administering retribution. The understanding that stoning is an ideal way to signal corporate retribution is also found in Greek sources, most notably in Plato's *Laws* (9.873b), where he suggests that the (already dead) criminal should be stoned by representatives on behalf of the entire city so that atonement be made for the whole city. It is also the case that in the literary topos of the persecuted prophet—a topos commonly employed in Hellenistic Jewish literature, on which Luke models his Stephen story—stoning is a typical means of inflicting punishment. Twice in the Hebrew Bible Moses is threatened with stoning (Exod 17:4; Num 14:9–10). Josephus includes both of these references and adds another in his account of Moses' trials (*Ant.* 3.12; 3.307; *Ant.* 2.327; cf. also *Ant.* 4.12). Zechariah, whose fate is so well known that he becomes the exemplum of the murdered prophet in Q/Luke 11:51, is also said to be stoned to death (2 Chr 24:21; cf. Josephus, *Ant.* 9.168).[30]

In contrast, stoning is not a Roman form of legal punishment. Theodor Mommsen's encyclopedic *Römisches Strafrecht* includes no entry on stoning. References to stoning in Roman literature depict it as something engaged in by the unruly mobs—those mobs so prone to violence and rage that are always threatening to tip out of control. Consider the mob conjured by Virgil in the *Aeneid* whose rage (*furor*) can only be calmed by a man of *auctoritas:*

> When rioting breaks out in a great city,
> And the rampaging rabble goes so far
> That stones fly, and incendiary brands—
> For anger can supply that kind of weapon—
> If it so happens they look round and see
> Some dedicated public man, a veteran
> Whose record gives them weight, they quiet down,
> Willing to stop and listen.
> Then he prevails in speech over their fury
> By his authority, and placates them.[31]

We are here, of course, back in the realm of imperial sociology. From this vantage point, the death of Stephen *by stoning* is perfectly un-Roman, perfectly barbarous.

Conclusion

One of the highest virtues exalted in narratives of Christian self-identity is the ability to forgive enemies. Such forgiveness is exemplified in the story of the stoning of Stephen, where Stephen's last words before dying at the hands of a Jewish mob are "Lord, do not hold this sin against them." Indeed it is because of these words attributed to Stephen in Acts that the church historian Eusebius memorializes Stephen as "the perfect martyr," the model for the succession of Christian martyrs who continued to pray for, and to forgive, those inflicting torture upon them. However, this

narrative of Christian self-identity, in which Stephen is presented as for-
giving the Jewish mob that torments him, is embedded in a text that does
nothing of the sort. The author of the book of Acts, unlike the protagonist
Stephen, shows no mercy in his dealings with Jews in his history of Christian origins.

In "Nietzsche, Genealogy, History," Foucault argues that the search
for the origins of a particular historical phenomenon implicitly posits
some essential identity, a primordial truth that precedes "the external
world of accident and succession."[32] The story of Stephen has functioned
in Christian interpretation as one of those originary, primordial truths. It
is a truth that reduces various agents to "essences," one Jewish and violent, the other Christian and violated. Both Luke and the church that
eventually adopted Luke's vision of earliest Christian history have told
this story as a means of constructing Christian identity against Judaism,
its Other. The powerful effects of such a story of violent originary separation explain the continued, unreflective certainty about its historicity.

Because of its canonical status and the mythic work that it does, the
story of the stoning of Stephen is not easily dislodged, neither in its power
nor its effects. As Robert Allen Warrior observed when contrasting
the story of the violent conquest of Canaan in the book of Joshua with
reconstructions of historical-critical biblical scholars, who posit a peaceful
infiltration of Canaan, "History is no longer with us. The narrative
remains."[33] This is as true for Stephen as it is for Joshua. But this does not
mean that historians can abnegate the responsibility of explaining how
the narrative comes into existence.

Notes

1. Christopher Mount demonstrates that the separation of these two volumes in the
canon, along with the distinguishing attributions "Gospel according to Luke" and "Acts
of the Apostles," owes to a late second-century construction of Christian origins that
compromises Luke's original narrative intentions. See his *Pauline Christianity: Luke-
Acts and the Legacy of Paul* (NovTSup 104; Leiden: Brill, 2002). While I would nuance
the relationship between Judaism and Christianity and the appeal to "Hellenistic literary
culture" in Luke-Acts somewhat differently than Mount does, on the whole Mount's
arguments are important and compelling. Observe especially his arguments for a late
dating of this work—somewhere in the early decades of the second century.

2. For a summary of recent scholarship on Acts' understanding of the relationship of
Christianity and Rome, see Gary Gilbert, "The List of Nations in Acts 2: Roman Propaganda and the Lukan Response," *JBL* 121, no. 3 (2002): 497–529, esp. 524–29. In my

view, Gilbert's argument that Luke-Acts expresses "opposition to the Roman empire" (528) and provides readers with "the tools to dismantle the ideological foundation upon which Rome has built its empire" (529) requires serious qualification in light of the favorable portraits of Roman officials and Roman institutions, especially in Acts. I suggest that the concept of mimicry as currently developing in the field of postcolonial criticism is useful for considering the paradoxical ways in which Luke-Acts both adopts, and also sometimes counters, Roman colonial ideology. (See Homi K. Bhabha, "Of Mimicry and Man: The Ambivalence of Colonial Discourse," in idem, *The Location of Culture* [London: Routledge, 1994], 85–92. In biblical studies, see Tat-siong Benny Liew's reading of Mark in his "Tyranny, Boundary, and Might: Colonial Mimicry in Mark's Gospel," *JSNT* 73 [1999]: 7–31.) Mimicry in colonial situations is never only simple imitation. I am developing the implications of this argument for reading Acts in my current research.

3. For general discussion of the links between Jesus, Stephen, and Paul, with bibliography, see Craig Hill, *Hellenists and Hebrews: Reappraising Division within the Earliest Church* (Minneapolis: Fortress Press, 1992), 59; Earle Richard, *Acts 6:1–8:4: The Author's Method of Composition* (SBLDS 41; Missoula, Mt.: Scholars Press, 1978), 281; David Moessner, "'The Christ Must Suffer': New Light on the Jesus—Peter, Stephen, Paul Parallels in Luke-Acts," *NovT* 28 (1986): 220–56. For discussion of Socratic models for Luke's narrative of the death of Jesus (and Stephen), see Greg Sterling, "*Mors philosophi*: The Death of Jesus in Luke," *HTR* 94, no. 4 (2001): 383–402. For identification of the Deuteronomistic motif of the persecuted prophets, see Odil Hannes Steck, *Israel und das gewaltsame Geschick der Propheten* (Neukirchen-Vluyn: Neukirchener Verlag, 1967); cf. also Hans-Joachim Schoeps, *Die jüdischen Prophetenmorde* (SymBU 2; Uppsala: Wretmans Boktryckeri, 1943); François Bovon, "La figure de Moïse dans l'oeuvre de Luc," in *La Figure de Moïse: écriture et relectures* (ed. Robert Martin-Achard et al.; Geneva: Labor et Fides, 1978), 47–65.

4. It is also possible that Luke intended to parallel the last words of Jesus and Stephen, who both forgive enemies (cf. Luke 23:34 and Acts 7:60). However, these words are absent from many early witnesses for Luke 23:34, and therefore cannot be established with certainty.

5. For a recent discussion of these charges, see Klaus Haacker, "Die Stellung des Stephanus in der Geschichte des Urchristentums," in *Aufstieg und Niedergang der römischen Welt: Geschichte und Kultur Roms im Spiegel der neueren Forschung* (ed. Hildegard Temporini and Wolfgang Hasse; II.26.2; Berlin: DeGruyter, 1995), 1515–53, esp. 1521–30.

6. Consider F. C. Baur's assessment of Stephen as "the most direct forerunner of the Apostle Paul" in *Paul, the Apostle of Jesus Christ, His Life and Works, His Epistles and Teachings: A Contribution to a Critical History of Primitive Christianity* (2 vols.; London: Williams & Norgate, 1873–75), 1.62; from *Paulus, der Apostel Jesu Christi: Sein Leben und Wirken, seine Briefe und seine Lehre* (2d ed.; 2 vols.; trans. A. P. Menzies [vol. 1] and A. Menzies [vol. 2]; Leipzig: Fues [L. W. Reisland], 1866–67). See also J. B. Lightfoot, "St. Paul and the Three" (originally published in 1865 in *Dissertations on the Apostolic Age* and reprinted [in the second and subsequent editions] of the author's *Saint*

Paul's Epistle to the Galatians (7th ed.; London: MacMillan & Co., 1881), 296–98. In twentieth-century scholarship, see, for example, Martin Hengel, "Between Jesus and Paul: The 'Hellenists,' the 'Seven,' and Stephen (Acts 6:1–15; 7:54–8:3)," in idem, *Between Jesus and Paul: Studies in the Earliest History of Christianity* (London: SCM, 1983), 1–29, esp. 24, 29.

7. For reconstructions of Stephen's Hellenistic, anti-law, anti-temple theology from charges in 6:11–14, see Baur, *Paul, the Apostle*, 1:52–53, 57–60. Alfred Loisy, *Les actes des apôtres* (Paris: E. Nourry, 1920), 309, 313–17; Hengel, "Between Jesus and Paul," 13, 22–24; Rudolf Pesch, *Die Apostelgeschichte* (2 vols; EKKNT 5:1–2; Neukirchen-Vlyun: Neukirchener, 1986), 1.238, 239; Richard, *Acts 6:1–8:4*, 288–89; James D. G. Dunn, *The Partings of the Ways* (Valley Forge, Pa.: Trinity Press International, 1991), 63–71. A useful review and critique of reconstructions of Stephen's Hellenistic theology based on these verses is supplied in Hill, *Hellenists and Hebrews*, 40–67.

8. For readings of Stephen's words in 7:47–50 as a rejection of the temple, see C. K. Barrett, "Attitudes to the Temple in the Acts of the Apostles," in *Templum Amicitiae: Essays on the Second Temple Presented to Ernst Bammel* (ed. William Horbury; JSNTSup 48; Sheffield: Sheffield Academic Press, 1991); Ernst Haenchen, *The Acts of the Apostles: A Commentary* (Philadelphia: Westminster, 1971), 290; Hans Conzelmann, *Acts of the Apostles* (Hermeneia; Philadelphia: Fortress Press, 1987), 56.

9. Helmut Koester, "GNOMAI DIAPHOROI: The Origin and Nature of the Diversification in the History of Early Christianity," in James M. Robinson and Helmut Koester, *Trajectories through Early Christianity* (Philadelpha: Fortress Press, 1971), 120. Cf. here Hill, *Hellenists and Hebrews*, 13.

10. See Hill, *Hellenists and Hebrews*, 9–11, for a summary of nineteenth-century critics of F. C. Baur.

11. Lightfoot, "St. Paul and the Three," 297–98. The close exegetical work of Hill in *Hellenists and Hebrews* on this question can now be contextualized by the broader theoretical studies of racial influences on nineteenth-century scholarship undertaken by Shawn Kelley in *Racializing Jesus: Race, Ideology, and the Formation of Modern Biblical Scholarship* (London: Routledge 2002); and Denise K. Buell in "Rethinking the Relevance of Race for Early Christian Self-Definition," *HTR* 94, no. 4 (2001): 449–76.

12. The recent cluster of arguments against the view of Stephen as radically rejecting law and temple includes Michael Bachmann, "Die Stephanusepisode (Apg 6,1–8,3): Ihre Bedeutung für lukanische Sicht des jerusalemischen Tempels und des Judentums," in *The Unity of Luke-Acts* (ed. J. Verheyden; BETL 142; Leuven: Leuven University Press, 1999), 545–62; H. Alan Brehm, "Vindicating the Rejected One: Stephen's Speech as a Critique of Jewish Leaders," in *Early Christian Interpretation of the Scriptures of Israel: Investigations and Proposals* (ed. Craig Evans and James A. Sanders; Sheffield: Sheffield Academic Press, 1997), 266–98; Haacker, "Die Stellung des Stephanus," 1521–39; Edvin Larsson, "Temple-Criticism and the Jewish Heritage: Some Reflexions on Acts 6–7," *NTS* 39 (1993): 379–95; Hill, *Hellenists and Hebrews*, 41–101; Peter Doble, "Something Greater Than Solomon: An Approach to Stephen's Speech," in *The Old Testament in the New Testament: Essays in Honour of J. L. North* (ed. Steve Moyise; JSNTSup 189; Sheffield: Sheffield Academic Press, 1991), 181–207; John J. Kilgallen,

"The Function of Stephen's Speech," *Bib* 70 (1989): 173–93; Dennis Sylva, "The Meaning and Function of Acts 7:46–50," *JBL* 106, no. 2 (1987): 261–75; Graham Stanton, "Stephen in Lucan Perspective," *StudBib* 3 (1978): 345–60.

13. For an argument that converges with mine in questioning the historicity of the Stephen episode, see Todd Penner, *In Praise of Christian Origins: Stephen and the Hellenists in Lukan Apologetic Historiography* (New York: T&T Clark, 2004). Unfortunately, this monograph appeared too late for me to take account of it here.

14. Baur, *Paul, the Apostle*, 38.

15. Eduard Zeller, *The Contents and Origin of the Acts of the Apostles Critically Investigated* (2 vols; Edinburgh: Williams & Norgate, 1875–1976), 1:237.

16. Hill, *Hellenists and Hebrews*, 101, my emphasis. This certainty about Stephen's death is standard fare also in more popular genres. In his reader on early Christianity, within the chapter entitled "Persecution and Martyrdom in the Early Church," Bart Ehrman cites the book of Acts as the oldest historical account and a clear indicator that "the earliest persecution of Christians was by Jews," and Acts 7:56–60 as record of the first Christian martyrdom (*After the New Testament: A Reader in Early Christianity* [Oxford: Oxford University Press, 1999], 25, 30). For critique of Ehrman's framework here, see Shelly Matthews, "Ethical Issues in Reconstructing Intra-Religious Violence in Antiquity: The Gospel of Matthew as a Test Case," in *Walk in the Ways of Wisdom: Essays in Honor of Elisabeth Schüssler Fiorenza* (Harrisburg, Pa.: Trinity Press International, 2003), 334–50, esp. 338–40. In James Carroll's popular and important history of the church and the Jews, he poignantly laments how the Gospels—and later the church—falsely impute onto "the Jews" responsibility for the death of Jesus. But then, in an unexamined move, the murder of Stephen by the Jews is placed in Carroll's narrative alongside the execution of Jesus under Pontius Pilate as one of the incontrovertible "facts" of this history (*Constantine's Sword: The Church and the Jews* [Boston: Houghton Mifflin, 2001], 70).

17. A most recent "dossier" on Stephen is supplied in François Bovon, "The Dossier on Stephen, the First Martyr," *HTR* 96, no. 3 (2003): 279–315. Bovon argues that the direction of his current research on Stephen calls into question the "unsubstantiated thesis" that there is no tradition on Stephen in the early church (287n48). But in the same article he notes that his own investigation, which he characterizes as still ongoing, has led him to conclude that silence on Stephen in the first century is matched by silence about Stephen in the following second-century sources: "The so-called Apostolic Fathers, the apologists, Justin Martyr, the early Christian Apocrypha, and the Nag Hammadi documents" (288). While Bovon has provided us with an impressive and important catalogue of references to Stephen in the early church after the time of Irenaeus, nothing from his near exhaustive search of sources can support the argument that Stephen's martyrdom is known in the early church before the end of the second century.

18. Ibid., 287–88.

19. On Irenaeus's use of Acts for defending a construction of Christianity based on a normative apostolic tradition correlated with a four-gospel canon and his role in rescuing Acts from obscurity, see Mount, *Pauline Christianity*, 11–29.

20. While Hebrews does not name its martyrs as Tertullian does, Tertullian's pairing of Isaiah, who is sawn in two, with Stephen, who is stoned to death, echoes the pairing of means of death in the martyrdom list of Heb 11:37: "they were stoned to death, they were sawn in two, they were killed by the sword; they went about in skins of sheep and goats, destitute, persecuted, tormented. . . ."

21. On this passage, see also John Marshall, *Parables of War: Reading John's Jewish Apocalypse* (ESJ 10; Waterloo, Ont.: Wilfried Laurier University Press, 2001), 58–59.

22. Lightfoot, "St. Paul and the Three," 298.

23. Cf. here the discussion in Erika Heusler, *Kapitalprozesse im lukanischen Doppelwerk: Die Verfahren gegen Jesus und Paulus in exegetischer und rechtshistorischer Analyse* (NTAbh 2.38; Münster: Aschendorffsche Verlagsbuchhandlung, 2000), 2–5.

24. Note that the tribune's motive is twice explained as his desire for *asphaleia*, 21:34; 22:30; cf. Luke 1:3.

25. Lawrence M. Wills, "The Depiction of the Jews in Acts," *JBL* 110, no. 4 (1991): 631–54, esp. 635. For a contemporary sociologist's reflection on how the dominant class perceives gatherings of the lower classes that converges with Wills's assessment, see James C. Scott, *Domination and the Arts of Resistance: Hidden Transcripts* (New Haven, Conn.: Yale University Press, 1990), 58–66.

26. Wills, "Depiction of the Jews," 653–54. As this quotation indicates, Wills also dates Acts into the second century. As he astutely perceives, Luke's depiction of Jews as repeatedly fomenting violence would fit well with what Roman overlords knew from the revolts of Egypt, Cyrene, and Cyprus (115–117 C.E.), and perhaps even the Bar Kokhba revolt in Palestine under Hadrian (132–135 C.E.). Cf. here also Mount, *Pauline Christianity*, 173n26. This argument about the portrayal of Jews as prone to mob violence serves as a rebuttal to arguments that Acts must be dated before the revolts under Trajan because Luke makes no explicit reference to them. See, for example, E. P. Sanders and Margaret Davies, *Studying the Synoptic Gospels* (London: SCM, 1989), 16–17.

27. For history of research on this question until 1982, see Heinz-Werner Neudorfer, *Der Stephanuskreis in der Forschungsgeschichte seit F. C. Baur* (Giessen: Brunnen, 1983), 277–83, 313.

28. Note Haenchen's commentary on 7:51–3: "Now the pack is unleashed to hunt Stephen out of the city and stone him. Probably here a part of the older Martyrdom emerges, and *it threatens to destroy the framework which Luke has so ingeniously, painstakingly constructed*: that of ostensibly legal proceedings before the High Council. . . . Hence Luke, by mentioning witnesses . . . *attempts to steer his account back into the paths of juridical procedure*" (*Acts of the Apostles*, 295–96, my emphasis). Cf. F. J. Foakes Jackson and Kirsopp Lake, *The Beginnings of Christianity Part I: The Acts of the Apostles* (5 vols.; London: Macmillan, 1920–33), 2.148–49; Hans Conzelmann, *Acts of the Apostles* (trans. James Limburg, A. Thomas Kraabel, and Donald H. Juel; Hermeneia; Philadelphia: Fortress Press, 1987), 61.

29. J. J. Finkelstein, *The Ox That Gored* (Transactions of the American Philosophical Society 71:2; Philadelphia: American Philosophical Society, 1981), 27. See also Rudolf Hirzel, "Die Strafe der Steinigung," *Abhandlungen der Philologisch-Historischen Klasse der Königlich sächsischen Gesellschaft der Wissenschaften* 27, no. 7

(1909): 223–66; Josef Blinzler, "The Jewish Punishment of Stoning in the New Testament Period," in *The Trial of Jesus: Cambridge Studies in Honour of C. F. G. Moule* (ed. Ernst Bammel; Naperville, Ill.: A. R. Allenson, 1970), 147–61.

30. For the motif of the persecuted prophet in the Hebrew Bible, see especially Neh 9:16–31; 2 Chr 36:11–21, and discussion in Steck, *Israel und das gewaltsame Geschick der Propheten*, 60–80, and in Melanie Johnson-DeBaufre's essay in this volume. Persecution of prophets is a theme common to the *Lives of the Prophets*, where six of the twenty-three named prophets are said to die by unnatural means, and the *Martyrdom and Ascension of Isaiah*, which narrates that Isaiah was sawn in two (cf. Heb 11:37b). For discussion of rabbinic elaborations on this theme, see H. A. Fischel, "Martyr and Prophet," *JQR* 37 (1946/47): 265–80; 363–86. Steck includes discussion of rabbinic as well as Muslim and later Christian elaborations, *Israel und das gewaltsame Geschick der Propheten*, 86–109.

On the violent death of Zechariah, cf. 2 Chr 24:17–22; Josephus, *Ant.* 168–69; *Liv. Pro.* 23; Luke 11:51; *Targum to Lamentations* 2:20; and *b. Git.* 57b. See Sheldon H. Blank, "The Death of Zechariah in Rabbinic Literature," *HUCA* 13 (1938): 327–45; Schoeps, *Die jüdischen Prophetenmorde*, 17–21; and Melanie Johnson-DeBaufre's essay in this volume. Because of the similarity of the fate of Zechariah and Stephen, it is intriguing to compare the accounts of their last words. Zechariah: "As he was dying, he said, 'May Yahweh see and avenge!'" (2 Chr 24:22c; cf. Josephus, *Ant.* 9.169); Stephen: "Then he knelt down and cried out in a loud voice, 'Lord, do not hold this sin against them'" (Acts 7:60ab).

On Jerusalem as the city that "stones the ones who are sent to it," see Q/Luke 13:34.

31. *Aen.* 1.201–10, trans. Robert Fitzgerald. Cf. Livy, 4.50.4–9; Horace, *Epod.* 5.99; Suetonius, *Cal.* 5. See also Josephus, *Ant.* 14.2, where he speaks of the practice of stoning as "savagery" (ὠμότης).

32. Michel Foucault, "Nietzsche, Genealogy, History," in *Language, Counter-Memory, Practice: Selected Essays and Interviews* (ed. Donald F. Bouchard; trans. Donald F. Bouchard and Sherry Simon; Ithaca, N.Y.: Cornell University Press, 1977), 139–64, esp. 142.

33. Robert Allen Warrior, "Canaanites, Cowboys, and Indians: Deliverance, Conquest, and Liberation Theology Today," in *The Postmodern Bible Reader* (ed. David Jobling, Tina Pippin, Ronald Schleifer; Oxford: Blackwell, 2001), 191; repr. from *Christianity and Crises* 49 (1989): 191. Cf. also the discussion in Regina M. Schwartz, *The Curse of Cain: The Violent Legacy of Monotheism* (Chicago: University of Chicago Press, 1997), 153–59.

8

Violence and Religious Formation:
An Afterword

DAVID FRANKFURTER

Violence between "Jews" and "Christians" in the First
Century C.E.

The essays in this volume provoke thought about violence and religious formation in three important dimensions. First, the authors' particular selection of first- or early second-century texts invites us to think comparatively across some of the earliest documents of the Jesus movement that all depict violence by outsiders against insiders. To what degree is Jewish aggression a common historical experience of the early groups, or a leitmotiv of early Christian literature? Second, we are invited to think historically about representations of violence: For what purposes did these legends serve? Did they reflect actual intersectarian tensions within the amorphous Judaisms of the first century? Did they reflect real lynchings and riots in the experience of Jesus believers? And third, we are invited to think thematically—beyond the particular historical experience of early Jesus believers and the enemies they constructed: How might legends of violence conform to, or articulate, certain patterns in the ways that developing religious communities establish their boundaries?

Twenty or thirty years ago, the topic of "violence among Jews and Christians" would have conjured a quite established historiographical picture: that is, the innocent, enthusiastic people of the Way finding themselves repeatedly bullied, persecuted, even massacred by Jews (joined sometimes by Romans) wherever they went to spread the Word. This picture, of course, is thoroughly Lukan; but it was variously extended on the basis of other canonical texts: Revelation, for example, where scholars such as R. H. Charles and Elisabeth Schüssler Fiorenza saw Jews and Romans together ganging up on "Christians";[1] and the Gospel of John, where J. Louis Martyn offered a scenario of post-Yavneh, orthodoxy-consumed rabbis violently purging their synagogues of Johannine Christians.[2]

But several decades of attention to literary motifs in early Christian literature have provided us with a better sense of how persecution could operate as a theme in a text—even as a form of biblical exegesis—that may or may not reflect real experiences. On the one hand, as Leonard Thompson showed well for the book of Revelation, images of persecution could function as a rhetorical trope with multiple associations for audiences of different eras.[3] Greater historical attention to the reconstruction of alleged persecutions, moreover, has revealed greater tolerance and confusion on the part of Roman authorities and far less religious cohesiveness among Jews than portrayed by Luke or later Christian authors. On the other hand, the social contours of devotion to Jesus not only emerged within the penumbra of Judaism, but took quite different shapes and directions in different parts of the Mediterranean world, such that a word like "Christian" becomes historically anachronistic and distorting for the identification of specific groups with roughly contiguous beliefs. Indeed, far from an identifiable religious minority sparking outrage and persecution wherever they went, Jesus believers struck outsiders as an amorphous element of Judaism—a group whose outrageous reputation for incest and cannibalism could scarcely be verified in local inquests.[4]

Obviously this is not to deny that there were sporadic instances of persecution or organized violence against and among certain Jewish and quasi-Jewish groups in antiquity—Jesus believers included. One has only to read Josephus's *Jewish War* to get a sense that intrasectarian violence and repression were rife in and outside Palestine. The dramatic, Jewish-led mob assaults on Jesus believers that pepper the book of Acts may stem from some actual incidents. Yet these incidents—if real—would have been much more complicated than the legends report, with their stock characters of angry Jewish lynch mobs, Paul the purist rabbi, and pacifist *christianoi*. Whatever violence may have actually taken place—by "Jews" against Jesus believers, or simply among Torah-adhering people about the centrality of Jesus—it is clear from the studies in this volume that the letters of Paul, the Gospels of Matthew, John, and Luke, and the book of Revelation cannot themselves be used as evidence for violence.

Violence and the Narcissism of Minor Differences

Overall, the contributions to this volume suggest that legends of Jewish violence against Jesus believers arose, circulated, and became inscribed in the course of the consolidation of an independent, Jesus-focused identity that could be constructed along various axes—halakic, as in Revelation; political, as in Matthew; or cosmic/anthropological, as in John. That is, legends of violence allowed a subset of Jews to feel different from other Jews by virtue of imagining themselves persecuted by those other Jews. Intriguingly, these insiders could construe their intimate enemies from within Jewishness, as in Matthew or Revelation (or Paul in Galatians 1), or they could relegate the term *Ioudaios* entirely to the enemy, as in John. No doubt there were regional and historical factors as well as social dynamics that contributed to these various polarities in self-definition. One such dynamic, to which Adele Reinhartz points, would be a situation of cognitive dissonance or frustration in the limitations of one's message. The insiders' commitment to an ideology cannot admit the ideology's intrinsic failure to win converts; hence, the infidels' resistance must be due to their cosmic antagonism, even their enthrallment to Satan.

But perhaps the most consistent social dynamic behind the imagination and even the precipitation of violence was the principle of the "narcissism of minor differences." This was Sigmund Freud's elegant formulation of the rage that arises from the sensation that small distinctions between self and other threaten overall unity.[5] It is not major differences but minor ones—that "shouldn't be there," that the Other has imposed on preexistent harmony—that trigger this rage. Georg Simmel and his student Lewis Coser formulated this principle for the analysis of social dynamics, especially social and sectarian conflict. In Simmel's terms, "the degeneration of a difference in convictions into hatred and fight ordinarily occurs only when there were essential, original similarities between the parties."[6] Even if there are many groups claiming roughly similar practices or ideas, it is only those closest to the "insiders"—the intimate enemies—who attract the most outright hostility. In some cases (for example, Matthew and Revelation), the defining ideology of the Jesus movement encompassed strict adherence to Torah and Jewish tradition at least as centrally as the comprehension of Jesus as Christ; hence the intimate enemy would be those who, in the name of Christ-oriented Jewish purity, might suspend core halakic values.[7] In other cases (such as Paul himself), the comprehension of Jesus as Christ formed the principal boundary marker; and those who might complicate it with halakic clarity could be viewed as principal opponents. And in still other recorded cases, divergent interpretations of such essential matters as Christ, "antichrist," hierarchy, prophecy, or the vast complexity of ritual purity would be viewed as threatening to a larger unity.

Such doctrinal squabbles are experienced in social, cosmic, and even somatic terms. Unity and harmony come down to group interest, not intellectual debate: "You foolish Galatians! *Who* [τίς] has bewitched you?" (Gal 3:1). Their ruptures are projected into apocalyptic timetables of satanic influence and false leadership: "False messiahs and false prophets will appear and produce great signs and omens, to lead astray, if possible, even the elect. . . . So, if they say to you, 'Look! He is in the wilderness,' do not go out. If they say, 'Look! He is in the inner rooms,' do not believe it" (Matt 24:24–26).[8] At the same time, as Mary Douglas has argued, the sectarian group's integrity—across members, marginal adherents, leaders, and rivals or mavericks—comes to be symbolized as a body that is acutely sensitive to any fissure, bleed, irritation, or infection.[9]

As at Qumran, the internecine rivals and opponents that emerge in such worlds earn the most polarizing of names: "false apostles, deceitful workers," ministers of Satan in disguise (2 Cor 11:13–15); "antichrists" (1 John 2:18–22); "evildoers" (Rev 2:2); "synagogue of Satan" (Rev 2:9; 3:9). But more importantly, they—the opponents—are imagined as the perpetrators of schism and persecution, not us: "they went out from us, but they did not belong to us; for if they had belonged to us, they would have remained with us" (1 John 2:19). From them comes "affliction" and "suffering," requiring "endurance" (Rev 2:9–10; 2:2–3). It is only at the end that God and his angels will "repay with affliction those who afflict you—those who do not know God and on those who do not obey the gospel of our Lord Jesus" (2 Thess 1:8).

This pastiche of Scripture serves not to homogenize the demonizations and conflicts of the early Jesus movement but to suggest some patterns in vilification among early Jesus groups that seem to conform to Simmel's principle. The apocalyptic sectarian world is one of stark polarities, imputed violence, fantasized vengeance, and monstrous opponents. Moreover, its imaginal world of "us" in resistance to "them" is supported and maintained socially through an insiders' discourse or private idiom capable of labeling everything ambiguous or threatening in readily comprehensible, if compressed, codes: *antichristos, pseudoprophētēs,* the man of *anomia* and *apēleia.* Second Thessalonians, Revelation, and the Johannine letters all assume such restricted codes, familiar and potent to insiders while at best mysterious to outsiders, in addressing the tensions and rivalries in their midst.

Again, it must be said, the contribution—even domination—of such social dynamics to the construction of self-defining group narratives does not gainsay particular historical situations of inequity, even persecution. The essays in this volume do tend to reject, on sound historical and literary grounds, the notion that identifiable incidents of Jewish violence against "Christians" lie behind the literary depictions of such violence. Yet the studies of Matthew (Carter), Revelation (Marshall), and Mark/Q (Horsley) attribute much of these texts' hostile, anxious rhetoric to the experience of Roman colonialism: the (Jewish, Jesus-oriented) authors are not so much victims of particular persecution as subalterns in a singularly repressive colonial regime. In the cases of Luke-Acts, John, and Paul, however, the literary impulse to represent a peripheral group—the "intimate enemy"—as directly hostile to insiders arises almost exclusively as an internal trope of self-definition. Indeed, the trope works both ways, conveying not only the "enemy's" wrath against "us" but also—as in 2 Thessalonians above—"our" fury against them, in the form of threats and apocalyptic vengeance. These rhetorical and sociological dynamics seem to transcend particular historical situations. It would seem that sectarian movements have the capacity to imagine themselves persecuted even in largely peaceful times and among various economic strata—to erupt in fear and vengeance over what to observers might be the smallest indignities.[10]

Functions of the Religious Representation of Violence: Some Propositions

We tackle this issue of images of "original" violence by Jews against Christians not only in a post-Holocaust era, but also in an age marked by genocidal massacres of Bosnian Muslims and Rwandan Tutsis and religio-political massacres of Indian Muslims by Hindus, of traditional Sudanese tribes by northern Muslims, and of traditional Catholic villages in Guatemala by soldiers under an evangelical Protestant president. We are also heirs to increased historical scrutiny of violence against African Americans following the Civil War, against Jewish communities in Europe during the Middle Ages and early modern period, and against American indigenous cultures under Spanish invasion. In virtually every one of these cases, accusations of violence—or of conspiracy to violence—against the group ultimately victimized have proved central to mobilizing official or mob slaughter and equally central to legitimating that slaughter in official lore. "Their" violence becomes a pretext for "ours."

This point about the often catastrophic effects of imputing violence and claiming historical persecution bears serious consideration. Historians have a duty to remind society of the violent injustices done openly to ethnic minorities, women, and children; yet they must also point out situations where, on dubious or nonexistent evidence, those same minorities have been themselves accused of atrocities: African-American men accused of raping white women, Jews accused of abducting and "ritually" bleeding Christian children for consumption, Rwandan Tutsis and Bosnian Muslims imagined as bloodthirsty rapists of "our" women.[11] For example, as the medievalist Gavin Langmuir has put it, the novel eleventh-century fantasy of Jewish "ritual murder" and abuse of the Eucharist "enabled people to believe that Jews were torturing Jesus in many places at the same time."[12] And each such accusation impels massive, often sadistic acts of revenge against the "perpetrating" minority group or its representatives. Legends of violence can thus lend the hegemonic culture the pretense of persecution and an identity as "victim," a situation that has repeatedly led to lynching, pogroms, and massacres.

We are then at a point where the modes of violence, the various permutations of violence in religion or as a religious expression, and images of violence as imputation against others require ever more nuanced analysis, comparison, and classification.[13] The topics broached in the essays in this volume address only one subcategory of the larger field—that is, the representation of others' violence in the generative stages of a religious movement. Here I intend to put their larger themes in some comparative light.

Legends of violence and "primal atrocities" against those we consider our cultural-religious ancestors contribute to boundary formation in situations of unclear religious identity; for these legends call "us" to identify with martyrs and against "persecutors." The Gospel of John certainly exemplifies this kind of boundary formation: Reinhartz demonstrates the literally cosmic clarity attained by configuring a hostile *Ioudaioi* against an anxious and amorphous body of insiders. But across religions we find similar patterns. The murder of Ali at Karbala is paradigmatic for Shi'ite Muslim identity; while in the United States, the rush to make Cassie Bernall of Columbine High School a martyr at the hands of nihilistic Goths (despite actual events) has carried the same function for many evangelical Christian families.[14]

The anxieties of identity formation may in some cases be so multivalent that the legends and imagery of violence will be used to convey conflict on several levels. In the book of Revelation, for example, violence is both imputed to and called down upon intimate enemies such as "Jezebel" and the "so-called Jews" as well as wider forces in the Roman Empire. As we tease out this imagery of violence, we find fantasies of vengeance, accusations of persecution, and elevation of martyrdom working in many directions to shore up the sectarian Jewish identity of some group in Asia Minor. This kind of polyvalent imagery of violence has also consumed certain contemporary religious sects like the Solar Temple, the Peoples Temple of Jonestown, and Aum Shinrikyo, all with explosive results. The experiences of violence claimed by the leader merge with violence imputed to outsiders, the violence felt necessary to discipline wayward insiders, the violence anticipated at some kind of end time struggle, and the purificatory violence that the group embraces as its responsibility in the cosmos.[15] Early Mormonism developed a martyrological tradition essential to its identity out of real incidents of persecution in the lives of its founders; but while reveling in martyrdoms, the early leaders also preached bloodthirsty sermons against outsiders, which exploded in an 1857 massacre of emigrant families.[16] These materials do suggest that groups with these ideas might indeed spark violence.

The legend of the stoning of Stephen in Luke-Acts further suggests that legends of violence can be directed for sheer rhetorical effect, consolidating an image of the Other as intrinsically violent for a situation already boundaried or polarized. Luke-Acts, Matthews argues, invokes Roman caricatures of barbarian justice to influence readers' negative opinions of Jews and Jewish culture. But we might expand this observation to include the ways in which an author or demagogue—in antiquity and since— might invoke preexisting notions of inhumanity, such as cannibalism, perverse sexuality, and child exploitation, to ramify the neutral distinctions that the audience already accepts.[17] The foreign or religious Other in one's social environment is revealed, by invoking ancient caricatures and atrocity legends, as a monstrous Other. Certainly Luke's proposition that, as it were, "These Jews among whom the Way started—they're really a bunch of thugs," carries considerably less inflammatory power than the medieval rumor that "those Jews living next door to you, with whom your children play and from whom you buy cloth, crave Christian children's blood for their Passover matzah." Still, in both cases, the depiction of violent inhumanity serves to clarify and polarize an otherwise ambiguous or tolerant social situation. Similar rhetorical efforts have exacerbated differences between Serbs and Bosnian Muslims, Hutu and Tutsi Rwandans, and even white and African-American men in the American south—differences exaggerated to a threatening degree through legends of sexual atrocity. The Other becomes a sexual monster, preying on "our" wives and daughters and attacking "our" moral system.[18]

Violence can also be, as Gager suggests for Paul, an idiom of self-presentation and personal predilection.[19] Individual leaders' preoccupation with violence may be a more widespread factor than we normally assume in the group construction of a persecuting "other." Paranoia, elevated boundaries, and violence in some recent apocalyptic groups have been traced to the pathology and preoccupations of their leaders.[20] The vengeful fantasies and images of violent outsiders in Revelation and the Gospel of John too may have derived from certain distinct personalities before becoming generalized to sectarian experience.

Indeed, for some religious enclaves preoccupied with the interpretation of ancient atrocities (or apocalyptic images of imminent atrocities), violence can become a group predilection, woven into self-understanding, although in fluctuating ways. The Q document's litany of wrongful mob executions performed by Israelite ancestors (Q/Luke 11:49–51), Johnson-DeBaufre shows, represents at one level an intellectual attempt to read current misfortunes under the Romans (perhaps including Jesus' crucifixion) within an ancient Jewish tradition of self-criticism revolving around legends of the prophets' murders. But the gruesome details of prophets' blood pouring out (ἐκκεχυμένον) shows that there is more than just distanced reflection on history here. Violence and gore have become not just the subject but the very matrix of meaningful history. The insiders are to experience violence in the present too as the essence of divine action and Jewish self-understanding.

I am skeptical of attempts to view such predilections for violent imagery—individual or collective—merely as internalizations or displacements of historical experiences of imperialist violence, as Johnson-DeBaufre, Horsley, Marshall, and Carter tend to suggest. One finds equally graphic preoccupations with violence among those in singularly privileged and protected positions as well, as Mel Gibson's 2004 movie *The Passion of the Christ* and Tim LaHaye and Jerry Jenkins's twelve-volume *Left Behind* series testify.

Interestingly, in the Q case, which derives from a Jewish tradition of identifying Israel's guilt, it is not at all clear that the author(s)—the

"in-group" imagining this sequence of murders—identifies himself with
the perpetrators of violence. Q's language is (except for the voice of
Sophia) all third- and second-person, opening up an important space for
interpreters, if not the author himself, to identify with the murdered
prophets as victims of a blindly brutal Israel, not with Israel itself. The
very ambiguity of this tradition—as a basis of collective self-blame or as a
myth of one's own persecution by an "outer" collective—probably itself
gave rise to the angry imputations of violence to Jerusalem crowds and
subsequently the Jewish population in later gospel literature. Hence a
marginal sectarian ideology is ramified and popularized as a rationale for
Jewish blood-guilt. Once again, sectarian predilections for violent imagery
with historically peculiar origins become systematic ideologies of martyrdom and revenge as they migrate out of their original contexts.

The above comprise some of the general functions of legends of perse-
cutory violence raised by early Christian materials. Clearly the most press-
ing issue for the authors of these texts was the articulation of identity and
integrity vis-à-vis Jewish culture. But the same legends and kinds of legends assume a different resonance in subsequent centuries. Christianity
gains hegemony; yet its leaders still seek to galvanize borders, spark mass
piety and pilgrimage, and revitalize the lurid traditions of violence from
an earlier time. Thus we can speak of further functions to legends of violence when the tellers are no longer emergent sectarians in conflict but
rather troubadours, friars, official readers of festival cycles, festival actors,
burghers, and lay rumormongers. I offer here three such functions for the
ongoing preservation of legends of violence:

- The retelling of legends of violence by some Other (Jews, Moors,
  Turks, heathens) has sanctioned ritual dramas: pilgrimages, Eucha-
  rists, and reenactments. Whereas some ritual dramas, such as
  that of Ali at Karbala, can be experienced in a "spiritual"—non-
  vengeful—mode, we might observe that some of these reenactments, such as the infamous German passion plays and ritual-murder
  plays, have often triggered mob attacks on Jewish communities.
  Anti-Muslim ideology was maintained in Serbia up to the early
  1990s through ecclesiastical retellings of the martyr-legend of
  Prince Lazar and through a famous nineteenth-century play, *The
  Mountain Wreath,* which modeled mass extermination as sacred
  revenge for the atrocities and ethnic pollution long imputed to
  Ottoman rule.[21] Audiences become absorbed by the imagery of

martyrdom, social polarization, cosmic rightfulness, and satanic injustice. Their sympathies are galvanized, intensified, allowed to merge with those of others. One leaves such a drama not an individual but a Serbian or German "son of persecution," a participant in national-ecclesiastical myth, and anxious to settle the injustices of the origin times.

- Legends of original violence, especially those that dwell on the spilling of blood or dismemberment, have often functioned as etiologies to sanction relics or shrines. Not only the stories of Jewish "ritual murder" and host desecration mentioned above, but also those extensive martyrologies read aloud in Coptic, Syriac, Greek, and other churches many centuries after the supposed events all had the principal function to situate the holy body as a relic "here in this shrine, in this village." Through these extensive sufferings at the hands of Romans or Persians (or iconoclasts or Muslims), a neutral and ambiguous local character becomes both Christian hero and font of healing blood. The now mythical persecution and sequence of tortures demarcate the martyr's power, and by extension, the present shrine's authority. A Christian or orthodox "communitas" arises between the physical shrine-structure observable in the landscape and the horrific injustices of the past.[22]

  Interestingly, martyrs' relics—as mediators and symbols of ancient injustices—can serve as rallying points for collective mobilization as well. If in the late first century Luke's account of the stoning of Stephen highlighted Jewish incivility, by the early fifth century the relics of Stephen then circulating around the empire (and presumably accompanied by lurid homilies) could so infuse a Christian town in Minorca, Spain, with the "memory" of his martyrdom and the Jews' injustice *in illo tempore* that a mob followed the bishop over to a nearby Jewish town to convert its people forcibly to Christianity.[23]

- Finally, legends of *meaningful* violence, such as martyrdom or purge, can make sense of real but ambiguous incidents of massacre or murder. The killing of Cassie Bernall at Columbine "recalls" the persecution of ancient Christians and therefore signals a new stage in the war Satan (or secularism) wages on all true Christians; isolated acts of violence by Bosnian (or Indian) Muslims become for the Serbian (or Hindu) demagogue the latest expression of their long-standing assault on Orthodox or Hindu culture; while "our" massacre of those villagers becomes a "preemptive defense" against their age-old conspiracy to destroy us. The sporadic and brutal massacres of Jews in Germany following the call to the first Crusade (1096) seem to have been inspired as revenge for the crucifixion of Jesus, a primal atrocity symbolized in the very Holy Sepulcher the crusading bands had set off to liberate. The mythical enmity of the Jews to Christ made local Jewish communities a "clearer," more proximate threat than distant Saracens.[24] Just as new incidents of violence against us can be assimilated to mythical persecutions and martyrdoms of the past, any new motivations to violence on our part become clarified as reenactments of ancient heroes or revenge for ancient injustices.

Conclusion

In legends of original violence and persecution, Elizabeth Castelli has argued, violence becomes an essential dimension of truth.[25] The story of violence reveals the truth of "our" self-definition, the truth of "our" practices or shrines or claims, the truth of "their" fundamental evil. In the early Christian materials addressed in this volume, the retelling of legends of some original violence or period of violence—committed against "us" by those "like us but [evidently] not of us"—plays a critical part in identity formation: specifically, the historical formation of a separate identity for certain Jesus believers in the penumbra of Jewish culture. "Jews" in these legends, or some construct of "Jews," are the persecutors, the rejecters, the antagonists who force "us" to recognize our essential difference. Tragically, the inscribing of this perspective in the Christian canon played its own essential part in legitimating violence against Jews throughout European history.

Notes

1. R. H. Charles, *A Critical and Exegetical Commentary on the Revelation of St. John* (2 vols.; Edinburgh: T&T Clark, 1920), 1:56, 58; Elisabeth Schüssler Fiorenza, *The Book of Revelation: Justice and Judgment* (Philadelphia: Fortress Press, 1985), 118–19, 194–95.

2. J. Louis Martyn, *History and Theology in the Fourth Gospel* (2d ed.; Nashville: Abingdon, 1979).

3. Leonard L. Thompson, "A Sociological Analysis of Tribulation in the Apocalypse of John," *Semeia* 36 (1986): 147–74; cf. David Frankfurter, *Elijah in Upper Egypt: The Coptic Apocalypse of Elijah and Early Egyptian Christianity* (Minneapolis: Fortress Press, 1993), chapter 6.

4. Cf. Pliny, *Ep.* 10.96–97.

5. Sigmund Freud, "The Taboo of Virginity" [1917], *Standard Edition* (London: Hogarth Press, 1957), 11:199; cf. idem, "Group Psychology and the Analysis of the Ego" [1921], *Standard Edition,* 18:101.

6. Georg Simmel, *Conflict and the Web of Group-Affiliations* (trans. Kurt H. Wolff and Reinhard Bendix; New York: Free Press, 1955), 48. Cf. Lewis A. Coser, *The Functions of Social Conflict* (New York: Free Press, 1956); Jonathan Z. Smith, "What a Difference a Difference Makes," in *"To See Ourselves as Others See Us": Christians, Jews, "Others" in Late Antiquity* (ed. Jacob Neusner and Ernest S. Frerichs; Chico, Calif.: Scholars Press, 1985), 44–48; and David Frankfurter, "Jews or Not? Reconstructing the 'Other' in Rev 2:9 and 3:9," *HTR* 94, no. 4 (2001): 403–25, esp. 412–16.

7. Cf. Anthony J. Saldarini, *Matthew's Christian-Jewish Community* (Chicago: University of Chicago Press, 1994); David C. Sim, *The Gospel of Matthew and Christian Judaism* (Edinburgh: T&T Clark, 1998). On Revelation, see Frankfurter, "Jews or Not?," 416–22.

8. See Frankfurter, *Elijah in Upper Egypt,* chapter 5.

9. Mary Douglas, *Natural Symbols: Explorations in Cosmology* (New York: Pantheon, 1982), 103–24.

10. See the essays in Thomas Robbins and Susan J. Palmer, eds., *Millennium, Messiahs, and Mayhem: Contemporary Apocalyptic Movements* (New York: Routledge, 1997).

11. On the lynching of African-American men, see, for example, J. William Harris, "Etiquette, Lynching, and Racial Boundaries in Southern History: A Mississippi Example," *AHR* 100 (1995): 387–410. On Jews, see, for example, R. Po-chia Hsia, *The Myth of Ritual Murder* (New Haven, Conn.: Yale University Press, 1988). On Rwanda: Christopher C. Taylor, *Sacrifice as Terror: The Rwandan Genocide of 1994* (Oxford: Berg, 1999). On Bosnia: Michael A. Sells, *A Bridge Betrayed: Religion and Genocide in Bosnia* (Berkeley: University of California Press, 1996). See also Sudhir Kakar, *The Colors of Violence: Cultural Identities, Religion, and Conflict* (Chicago: University of Chicago Press, 1996), and Garry Wills, "The Dramaturgy of Death," *New York Review of Books,* May 21, 2001, 6–10.

12. Gavin I. Langmuir, "At the Frontiers of Faith," *Religious Violence between Christians and Jews: Medieval Roots, Modern Perspectives* (ed. Anna Sapir Abulafia; New York: Palgrave, 2002), 151.

13. Cf. Mark Juergensmeyer, *Terror in the Mind of God: The Global Rise of Religious Violence* (3d ed.; Berkeley: University of California Press, 2003); Bruce Lincoln, *Holy Terrors: Thinking about Religion after September 11* (Chicago: University of Chicago Press, 2003); and Stephen J. Stein, "The Web of Religion and Violence," *RelSRev* 28, no. 2 (2002): 103–8.

14. Justin Watson, *The Martyrs of Columbine: Faith and the Politics of Tragedy* (New York: Palgrave, 2002); see also Elizabeth Castelli, *Martyrdom and Memory: Early Christian Culture-Making* (New York: Columbia University Press, 2004), chapter 6.

15. See Robbins and Palmer, *Millennium, Messiahs, and Mayhem.*

16. Will Bagley, *Blood of the Prophets: Brigham Young and the Massacre at Mountain Meadows* (Norman: University of Oklahoma Press, 2002), on which see Caroline Fraser, "The Mormon Murder Case," *New York Review of Books,* November 21, 2002, 18–23. See also Jon Krakauer, *Under the Banner of Heaven* (Garden City, N.Y.: Doubleday, 2003).

17. Cf. M. J. Edwards, "Some Early Christian Immoralities," *Ancient Society* 23 (1992): 71–82; Andrew McGowan, "Eating People: Accusations of Cannibalism Against Christians in the Second Century," *JECS* 2 (1994): 413–42; James B. Rives, "Human Sacrifice Among Pagans and Christians," *JRS* 85 (1995): 65–85; and Gustav Jahoda, *Images of Savages: Ancient Roots of Modern Prejudice in Western Culture* (London: Routledge, 1999).

18. See sources above, n. 11.

19. See also Robert Hodgson, "Paul the Apostle and First-Century Tribulation Lists," *ZNW* 74 (1983): 59–80.

20. Jim Jones of the Peoples Temple, Shoko Asahara of Aum Shinrikyo, and Jo Dimambro and Luc Jouret of the Solar Temple are notable cases.

21. Cf. Sells, *A Bridge Betrayed,* chapter 2.

22. See in general Hsia, *The Myth of Ritual Murder*; Miri Rubin, *Gentile Tales: The Narrative Assault on Late Medieval Jews* (New Haven, Conn.: Yale University Press, 1999), esp. 89–92. On Coptic martyrdoms and the sanctioning of relic-shrines, see Violet MacDermot, *The Cult of the Seer in the Ancient Middle East* (London: Wellcome Institute, 1971). In general, see David Frankfurter, "On Sacrifice and Residues: Processing the Potent Body," in *Religion in Cultural Discourse* (ed. Brigitte Luchesi and Kocku von Stuckrad; Berlin: De Gruyter, 2004), 511–33.

23. See Scott Bradbury, ed., *Severus of Minorca: Letter on the Conversion of the Jews* (Oxford: Oxford University Press, 1996). Among Stephen homilies with the potential to inflame audiences against the Jews, see especially that of Asterius of Amasea (c. 400 C.E.), in Johan Leemans et al., *"Let Us Die That We May Live": Greek Homilies on Christian Martyrs from Asia Minor, Palestine, and Syria* (c. A.D. 350–A.D. 450) (trans. B. Dehandschutter; London: Routledge, 2003), 176–84, esp. 181–82 (chapters 9–10).

24. Cf. Robert Chazan, "The Anti-Jewish Violence of 1096: Perpetrators and Dynamics," in *Religious Violence between Christians and Jews: Medieval Roots, Modern Perspectives* (ed. Anna Sapir Abulafia; New York: Palgrave, 2002), 21–43, esp. 35–36.

25. Castelli, *Martyrdom and Memory,* 193–96.

CONTRIBUTORS

—————

Warren Carter is Pherigo Professor of New Testament at Saint Paul School of Theology, Kansas City, Missouri, and is the author of *Pontius Pilate: Portraits of a Roman Governor, Matthew and Empire: Initial Explorations,* and *Matthew and the Margins: A Socio-Political and Religious Reading.*

David Frankfurter, author of *Elijah in Upper Egypt* and *Religion in Roman Egypt: Assimilation and Resistance,* is Professor of Religious Studies and History and Director of the Religious Studies Program at the University of New Hampshire.

John G. Gager has taught at Princeton since 1968. His scholarly concern is with the religions of the Roman Empire, especially early Christianity and its relations to ancient Judaism. He has also written on the theme of religion and magic. His books include *Moses in Greco-Roman Paganism, Kingdom and Community: The Social World of Early Christianity, The Origins of Anti-Semitism, Curse Tablets and Binding Spells from the Ancient World,* and *Reinventing Paul.*

E. Leigh Gibson is an independent scholar based in Princeton, New Jersey, who has taught at Oberlin College and Rutgers University. She is also the author of *The Jewish Manumission Inscriptions of the Bosporan Kingdom.* She and Shelly Matthews initiated the SBL Consultation on Violence and Representations of Violence among Jews and Christians.

Richard A. Horsley is Distinguished Professor of Liberal Arts and the Study of Religion at the University of Massachusetts, Boston, the author of many books, and the editor of *Paul and the Roman Imperial Order, Paul and Empire: Religion and Power in the Roman Imperial Society,* and *Paul and Politics: Ekklesia, Israel, Imperium, Interpretation.*

Melanie Johnson-DeBaufre is Assistant Professor of Religion at Luther College. She is the co-editor of *Walk in the Ways of Wisdom: Essays in Honor of Elisabeth Schüssler Fiorenza,* and the author of *Jesus Among Her Children: Q. Eschatology and the Construction of Church Origins.*

John W. Marshall teaches Early Christianity in the Department for the Study of Religion at the University of Toronto.

Shelly Matthews is Associate Professor of Religion at Furman University, the co-editor of *Walk in the Ways of Wisdom: Essays in the Honor of Elisabeth Schüssler Fiorenza,* and the author of *First Converts: Rich Pagan Women and the Rhetoric of Mission in Early Judaism and Christianity.*

Adele Reinhartz is Dean of Graduate Studies and Research at Wilfrid Laurier University, Waterloo, Ontario, where she is also Professor in the Department of Religion and Culture. She has written extensively on the Gospel of John.

INDEX